Le Bouc Demons of Camerone

by

Ian Colquhoun

ISBN: 978-1-326-00747-8

www.publishnation.co.uk

About The Author

Ian Colquhoun is a severely disabled author and historian from Livingston, Scotland. This is his 9th book. He lost his legs and was almost killed in an unprovoked arson attack in Ireland when he was just 24 years old. Prior to losing his legs, Ian worked in warehousing. He studied history at The University of Edinburgh.

www.iancolquoun.org.uk

Acknowledgments

The following people helped make this wee novel happen, either by direct assistance, advice, support, inspiration, encouragement, help with other things or simply friendship. 'Thank You' to...

The brilliants artists - May Yang, Martin Symmers, Chris Wainwright and John Colquhoun.

The Historian, Dr Michael Hogan of Guadalajara, Mexico.

Mum, Dad, Angela W, David W, Davie 'Disco' McDermott, Tony 'Mad Dog' Diuers, Jenny of Hood, Maggie McDermott, Pauline McDermott, John Norton, Uncle Ronnie, John Abbey, Kath Pete and Adrian, Alan Abbey, Willie Colquhoun, Dr Chris Brown, Steve Richards, David Morrison, Michael and Sara, Alex Salmond MSP, Ian Murray MP, Angela Constance MSP, Owen-Dudley-Edwards, Sir Tom Farmer, Brian Warfield, Tommy Byrne, Noel Nagle, Jimmy and the rest of the 'boys', Stevie Dodds, Jim Slaven, Jason Hool, John and Kim, Debbie Hall, Lynn Nelson, the late James Loughran (RIP), Brian O'Rourke, Paddy Mangan, Sandra Dick, Anna-Maria Diamond, Simon Keane, Keith Russell, Gerry Regan, Joe Gannon, the brothers O'Donnell, Laurie Burgi, Sarah Don, my fans, family, comrades and many others too numerous to mention. God Bless you all.

To my nephew, Ewan Wynne. God Bless You

This book is dedicated to the memory of all the brave soldiers of France's Foreign Legion and Regular Army who fell in the Mexican War of the 1860's, and also to the memory of the brave Mexican soldiers who fought and died in the conflict, no matter which side they fought on. Death does not discriminate – neither does heroism. Poor men fight rich men's wars. The Camerone story deserves a movie, and a decent documentary. For my part, with this book, all I wanted to do was bring the Camerone story to life, in the English language. I first read about the basic story when I was an able-bodied teenager, now, as a double-amputee man in my 30's, I'm honoured to tell a story that features one of history's most famous amputees. Ironically, my interest in Camerone was rekindled when in 2010 I did some work as a stunt-model on a multi-national medical exercise, and on the job I got talking to a serving Legionnaire, about Camerone. He was surprised and impressed that I knew about it, I was encouraged by his enthusiasm about the battle.

I decided there and then that I would write a wee novel about Camerone – I may not have started it right away, but, as usual, I kept the idea 'in my pocket', until now. Remember though – this is a novel – not a factual reference book.

Writing is my only escape from Injustice and Post Traumatic Stress Disorder. Writing Sets Me Free.

"From little towns in far lands we came,
to save our honour and a world aflame.
By little towns in far lands we sleep,
and trust the world we won, for you to keep"

At some point in your life, you may be in a bar or public place somewhere and you may hear a group of men singing a very silly song in French about sausages. In English, these are the lyrics:

Here you are, some blood sausage, some blood sausage, some blood sausage
For the Alsatians, the Swiss, and the Lorrains,
For the Belgians, there's none left,
For the Belgians, there's none left,
They're lazy shirkers.
For the Belgians, there's none left,
For the Belgians, there's none left,
They're lazy shirkers.

In French, it'll say this:
Tiens, voilà du boudin, voilà du boudin, voilà du boudin
Pour les Alsaciens, les Suisses et les Lorrains.
Pour les Belges y en a plus.
Pour les Belges y en a plus.
Ce sont des tireurs au cul.
Pour les Belges y en a plus.
Pour les Belges y en a plus.
Ce sont des tireurs au cul.

It's not a novelty song – I wouldn't advise that you mock those singing it.

Chapter One – Mick's Story

1860. Ireland

My name is Michael Warfield. Life was once so simple.

We had our little farm, a few pigs, some chickens, some potatoes and cabbages always on the go – and above all, we had each other. My family was never rich, not even well-off, but we survived, and took great pride in working our own little allotment of land. We relied on no-one else for help, and we did our best to help out any of our neighbours if they were ever struggling. It was a hard life, but a wholesome one. We had a few acres of land and a one-storey, single-roomed cottage with a thatched roof, just outside Sligo in Ireland. My mother had died bringing me and my twin sister Siobhan into the world in 1839, but I had my older brother Patrick, 5 years my senior, Siobhan, and of course, we had my old Da. We raised our meagre amount of crops and looked after our animals, sometimes selling a pig on market day to help make ends meet. We had an English landlord, a lovely man called Mr. Graves who gave us no trouble and was understanding and helpful if and when we were sometimes a little bit late with the monthly rent. He never threatened us with eviction, and even helped us out sometimes when my brother, sister, Da or I needed to see a doctor. It may sound like a mundane existence, and we all missed our Ma terribly, especially Da, but we just made the best of things and got on with it. Mr. Graves and his wife even provided free schooling for us, and for the children of their other tenants. We were happy, it was all we knew, and for the first seven years of my life, that was my world. My blissful, simple world. Then in 1846, The Great Famine came and nothing was ever the same again.

The potato blight reached our little piece of the world in 1846, turning our most important crop and the cornerstone of all our meals into inedible sludge. Hundreds of thousands of people died in Ireland, while still hundreds of thousands more fled the famine by taking passage on the coffin ships. As a family, we decided to stay, but the devastation of the crop meant that sooner or later, we would have to make changes. Mr. Graves took pity on our plight, and those of our neighbours, and simply 'forgot' to collect his rent for almost six months. He wasn't like the other landlords- he was a genuinely nice man. I think that if he had lived longer, my life would have been very different.

With his help, and a little bit of help from our Catholic priests, we managed to survive The Great Famine without resorting to becoming 'Soupers'- Protestant English Missionaries were roaming the Island, offering soup as famine relief, but only on the condition that those 'soup-takers' renounced their faith and became Protestants, in exchange for a simple bowl of soup. As my sister Siobhan and I got older, we were able to do a lot more to help our Da and big brother Patrick on our little farm. By my 20th birthday in 1859, things were looking up for our wee family. Neither my brother or I had been forced to take what was for many young Irishmen the only job going – joining the British Army – as we made enough pennies from the farm and from the extra work that Patrick and I did for Mr. Graves, building walls out of stones on his own personal land. Siobhan also worked in Mr. Graves' household, cleaning mostly. Siobhan was so beautiful, and Patrick and I were big and strong. On the other hand, by 1860, Da was failing.

His breathing deteriorated to the point that he was virtually bedridden. Mr. Graves' doctor told us that Da was suffering from Consumption (Tuberculosis) and that there was very little that we could do. However, such was life back in Ireland, Da was a good age at 51 by then, and he seemed to take solace in us, his children.

Then, in August of 1860, just before harvest time, Mr. Graves died. We were greatly saddened by his loss, and his funeral was well-attended by both landlords and tenants, English and Irish. The great turn-out at his funeral led us to assume that he would be replaced by a similar man, or perhaps by one of his family members – how wrong we were.

Within two weeks of Mr. Graves' funeral, we had a new landlord. Not another English one, but an Irishman from Dublin by the name of Sweeney. It didn't take Mr. Sweeney long to show us his true colours. Soon after he arrived, Siobhan came home from working at his house one evening, she was in tears and her shawl was ripped.

She told us that Mr. Sweeney had attempted to bed her, and that when she had refused him he had exploded in a vile rage, telling her 'you and those brothers of yours shouldn't bother coming back here to look for work'. Patrick and I were enraged and wanted to pay this fat Dubliner a visit that very night, landlord or no landlord, but our father counselled caution.

'We still have the farm now, it'll be alright, we can manage, just stay out of his way for now' he said. Da's optimism was to prove at best, misguided and at worst, deluded.

Chapter Two – The Landlord

The next morning, the four of us were eating our breakfast when Da suffered an unusually bad bout of coughing. It was like he was vomiting blood, and it broke our hearts that there was nothing we could do about it. We knew he didn't have long left. We were comforting Da when we heard a horse's hooves outside our little home, followed by a menacing shout of 'Warfield, get out here!'

Patrick told Siobhan to stay indoors, then gestured me to join him outside, where we were confronted by the sight of the fat Mr. Sweeney mounted on a bay horse, with four big tough-looking badly-dressed men, all carrying truncheons, at his side.

Mr. Sweeney spoke first.

'Where's your father? I have important news for him'.

Patrick answered.

'He's not well at all, I can speak for him'.

'Can you now?' said Sweeney with a sneer. 'Well I'll get straight to the point. I was having a look through Mr. Graves' old paperwork, and it seems you owe me a fair few pound. Six month's rent, plus interest, going back to 1847, and I want that debt settled now.'

Patrick and I were stunned. We had owed this money to Mr. Graves, not Sweeney, and we had certainly never expected to have to pay it back. But there was more, as Sweeney continued.

'If you don't give me my money today, my boys here will evict you today. It's all legal and there's nothing you can do about it.'

I made to lunge towards Sweeney but Patrick, always the calmer, more responsible one, grabbed my arm, stopping me, and then he tried to reason with Sweeney, whilst hiding his anger over his earlier assault on our sister.

'Look here Mr. Sweeney, we harvest in a few weeks and we take our livestock to market. We can give you some of the money then, but even with that, it's gonna be impossible for us to pay you such a vast amount of back-rent unless you let us pay in yearly instalments. Given what you tried to do to my little sister last night, I think that's

4

a fair deal. We're good tenants, we've been here for years, you'll get your bloody money, Mr. Graves never had any problem with...'
Sweeney interrupted.

'Mr. Graves is dead now, I'm the landlord here now, and I'll do as I please with my own land and tenants. Who's going to stop me?' Sweeney nodded towards his four hired thugs, who laughed, before Sweeney continued.

'I suppose I could maybe accept deferred payment and an increase in your rent, which would mean you could stay, as long as that lovely wee sister of yours spends tonight up at my house'.

I was surprised at Patrick's calmness at Sweeney's last statement, but I followed his lead, as I always did. Patrick, appearing to be considering this vile 'deal' ,asked Sweeney if he would give us a few moments to discuss things in our house, which Sweeney agreed to, with the caveat that we didn't 'take too long as he had many other tenants to visit today.' Patrick and I went inside.

Da and Siobhan had heard every word. They told us to tell Sweeney and his hired toughs to go to the devil, but then Patrick spoke to us.

'We've a problem here, so we have. On the one hand we should all go out there and tear that fat piece of shit to ribbons for what he tried to do to Siobhan. On the other hand, though it's a shitty thing he's done about our old rent, we haven't a leg to stand on legally. That bastard has the law on his side, and with it, the Sheriffs, the Bailiffs and even the soldiers. I was talking to Jim Hogan in the Shebeen (pub) a few nights ago and he says this Sweeney's been at the same game with all the tenants, and our Siobhan's not the only local young one he's got his eye on. '

I asked Patrick if we should put Sweeney off until tomorrow, then we could go round the area tonight gathering support from the other tenants, then we could confront him the next day as one group, stronger together. Patrick was about to answer when Da joined in, speaking slowly between blood-filled gurgling coughs.

'Listen here now, this kind of landlord is all over Ireland now, even in parts of The North. It's been coming for a while. These new Dublin money men are even worse than the English. They want everybody off the land so that they can keep sheep and other cattle on it instead, they make more money that way. We can't be uniting with the other tenants though – as soon as Sweeney gets wind of anything like that he'll go running to the Sheriff claiming that we're trying to start a rebellion, soldiers will come, there'll be trouble and we'll every one of us be evicted. That's just what Sweeney wants.'

I asked Da and Patrick what must be done and reminded them that we had been personally insulted by Sweeney's attack on Siobhan. Then we heard Sweeney shouting arrogantly from outside 'hurry up now, and boys, tell that sister of yours to put a bit more effort in in bed tonight than she did last night, no man likes to lie with a crying statue'.

We all looked at Siobhan. At first she stared at the ground, then looked at us all, and then she started to stare at nothing, in silence, as tears rolled down her beautiful face. We immediately knew that she had lied to us – Sweeney had raped her, but Siobhan had chosen to conceal it from us as she probably knew how we would react – angrily. Angry wasn't even the word, there isn't a word in that feckin' English language to describe how angry we were. For a moment we were all silent, and then Da spoke.

'Patrick, drag that old chest out from underneath my bed'.

Patrick dragged out the plain wooden box from under Da's bed, just as I saw Da cough another load of blood into the rag he was using as a handkerchief. We could all see that Da was dying. When Patrick had opened the box – a box that none of us had ever been allowed to look into before- Da spoke again before Patrick could remove the dust-cover which concealed the items in the chest.

'My beautiful children, I'm dying, I'll not see out the week. Know that me and your departed mother have and will always love you. I'll be with her very soon, so what happens to me is not important – but what happens to you three now is everything. Get as far away from this place as you can. Run. Go to America or England. In days of old I'd have sent you to join France's Irish Brigade perhaps, but those days are long gone. Paddy, my oldest boy, my shining star, take your brother and your sister and get away from here, but before you go, give this Sweeney fella his answer. You'll find that answer in my own Da's old chest there.'

'I will Da' said Patrick.

That was the first time I had ever heard Da call Patrick 'Paddy'. Together, Patrick and I examined the old box's contents. Inside the box was an old half-pike, like the kind used by the Rapparee soldiers back in the 1600's. There was also what looked like a British Army bayonet, a Blunderbuss, and two rifled flintlock pistols, plus eight cartridges. The box also contained some outdated gold French Livres. Da spoke again.

'Those aren't duelling pistols, they're rifled, better accuracy. Load them now boys, and the Blunderbuss. Paddy, you're the strongest, you take the Pike, Michael, you take the bayonet.'

We did as our father asked and then, without any further prompting, Patrick and I turned to go outside, just as Sweeney shouted 'Well, what's it to be, you scum?'. Siobhan stayed indoors with Da and we each grabbed a pistol and stuck them in our belts before walking through the door.

Of course, there was only ever going to be one reaction from us after we realised what that fat bastard Sweeney had did to Siobhan. Patrick and I charged out of the door, roaring, and two of Sweeney's hired thugs turned tail and ran away in terror straight away. Our family's honour had been impugned and though we knew that the law would catch up with us, that didn't stop us. We wanted to send a message to landlords like Sweeney, and we wanted to kill Sweeney himself.

The two heavies who stayed to fight us were the Lawlor twins, big, oafish brutes that drank in the local Shebeen and who would fight anyone for money, or even for a drink. They were no match for two enraged brothers defending their family honour. Patrick easily parried a truncheon blow by the larger of the twins, then hacked the brute from the shoulder almost down to the heart with one stroke of the half-pike. The man collapsed dead instantly just as his brother caught me on the head with a truncheon blow, but before he could strike me again, Patrick blew his brains out with his pistol, splattering my face with the man's brains and blood. Then I heard an unexpected second shot.

Mr. Sweeney had retreated some yards upon seeing two of his hired thugs run away and another one cut in half, and with no stomach for a hand-to hand fight himself, the fat oaf had produced a revolver from his saddlebag and shot my brother Patrick in the stomach, disabling him but not killing him. Sweeney then pointed his revolver at me. I ignored his warning to 'stay still' as I knew that I had to take him down or he would be able to murder my whole family, but he had the advantage, until a third loud bang rang out and blew the revolver from his hand, mangling his right arm and peppering his torso in the process .

He screamed like a stuck-pig and his cries of pain were like music to my ears. In a flash, Sweeney grabbed his horse's reins with his left hand, turned about, then rode off back towards his estate, slumped in the saddle. I looked behind me, relieved to be alive, and to my disbelief I saw my twin sister Siobhan, standing in the doorway, crying, holding a still-smoking Blunderbuss. I should have shot Sweeney down with my own pistol, but my concern was for Patrick, who was groaning in agony on the ground.

Without saying a word, Siobhan and I picked up our big brother and carried him inside. We laid him out beside Da. Patrick then spoke, his voice very weak, and I knew from the trail of blood on the ground where we had carried him back into the house that he was going to die. We examined his wound – that bastard Sweeney had deliberately shot him in the stomach, as it usually takes days for a man to die from such a wound – but Mr. Sweeney was no marksman, and had clearly fired too high into Patrick's body.

Of course this was no consolation to any of us – either way, Patrick was going to die. I spoke to him.

'I'm sorry Patrick, I'm so sorry, brother'.

Patrick spoke, faintly. 'Now you've got nothing to be sorry for Michael, we upheld our honour and stood up for ourselves, now you and Siobhan, be off with ya – that bastard Sweeney will be back with the Sheriff and a platoon of soldiers by nightfall.'

I protested to my big brother and pointed out that we couldn't leave him and Da to the mercy of the redcoats, but then Da spoke.

'Now listen, Michael, your brother and I are finished, we'll be with your mother in a few hours. You and your sister have to run. America, England, anywhere. No-one will believe us over a right-wing souper like Sweeney anyway, it's no use you hanging son. Take the gold coins from the chest – they're old but they're gold, there should be enough there to get passage on a ship. Go south first. The family must survive, son.'

Siobhan then spoke, refusing point-blank to leave our father and brother untended, but imploring me to go. I couldn't refuse my sobbing sister and my dying father and brother, so reluctantly, I agreed to leave the three of them and run away. I loaded the pistols and the Blunderbuss for them, took the gold coins, and then embraced my little family for the last time. They all spoke to me in turn before I left.

Da reminded me once more never to forget my family, and never to blacken my honour.

Patrick said two things to me. He whispered to me that he had always thought that I would be the famous brother, then he said aloud 'we sure gave them Lawlor twins a good battering didn't we?'

He laughed then coughed up more blood. My face was wet with tears, then Siobhan spoke to me for the last time.

'Don't worry about me, Michael, the soldiers are better behaved than Sweeney and his thugs.'

I didn't believe her, but we embraced again, and I walked out of the door of our family home for the last time.

As Da had advised, I headed down south to Galway to find a boat, rather than trying to board one in Sligo, as the soldiers and Sheriff's men would no doubt have been looking for me there. After a week's journey and resting, I plucked up the courage to board a ship bound for America, the passage used up about half of the gold that I had. As things turned out, my fellow passengers and I were conned.

The ship's captain was a crook, and rather than taking us across the Atlantic to the land of opportunity, he simply sailed due west from Galway before coming about to the north-east. Of course, none of us passengers realised what was going on until it was too late, all we could see was sea so it never occurred to us that we were going in the wrong direction. After two weeks at sea, we sighted land, but it soon became apparent to us that the ship's captain had defrauded us. Instead of sailing into New York, we docked at Leith, Edinburgh, in Scotland. I had fallen for one of the oldest tricks in the book, but rather than take it up with the captain, I simply disembarked at Leith, hoping to make myself a new life in Edinburgh – a city that I knew nothing about in a country that I also knew nothing about.

All through that arduous journey across Ireland to Galway and then over the sea to Scotland, I was a troubled man. Though I knew that I was practically safe from the law in Ireland, the fate of my family hung heavily on my conscience. They had given me no choice but to leave, but that hadn't made it any easier. I thought that I should have stayed behind to fight the redcoats when they came, however futile that may have been. I knew that my beloved brother and father were dead, and that that bastard Sweeney had probably taken possession of our land, but worst of all, I worried about my twin sister Siobhan. Had she been raped by the soldiers? Or by Sweeney and his men? Had she and my dying family fought on with what few munitions they had? I simply didn't know. At the very least, Siobhan would be in jail – if the Sheriff had been merciful.

My gold lasted me a couple of months in Edinburgh, I explored the city and stayed with a family in modest lodgings with all the other Irish immigrants in the city's Cowgate. The slums in the Cowgate, dubbed 'Little Ireland' by locals, were breeding grounds for disease and poverty – but at least I was safe there. As 1861 dawned, I was running out of money and running out of hope. Jobs for Irishmen were few and far between, even with my experience as a builder of walls and as a farm-hand. As my fortunes began to fade, I dwelled even more so on my behaviour back in Ireland. I began to see myself as a coward, a low-life, a man who had no honour and who had dishonoured his family. My dreams were even worse. All I could see in them was Siobhan's tearful face as I had left them. I was a dishonourable coward. Spring found me missing my family so badly that I was contemplating suicide. Then, something happened. Whilst out 'walking about' looking for work, I saw a sign in a tavern window on the High Street which read 'help required' , but unlike most similar signs in Edinburgh, it didn't say 'No Irish Need Apply' at the bottom. It turned out that the tavern was being used by a local builder to recruit men for public building works in the town. That builder's name was Jim Reid, the same age as me, but a tall 'six-footer' with brown hair and a facial scar, and meeting him in that tavern changed my life forever.

Chapter Three – Jimmy's Tale

1861. Edinburgh

I liked Michael Warfield from the very first time that I met him in 1861 when he came into the tavern looking for work. I'd always had a lot of time for the Irish, despite the hysterical anti-Catholic and anti-Irish prejudice which seemed to infect much of Scotland for no apparent reason. That's not to say that I trusted him from the start, but we got on well and soon became good friends. He never told me why he was in Scotland, and I never asked. He was a big strong, and literate young man, the same age as me, 21 or 22, about five –feet and eight inches tall, with red hair, and as I was looking for labourers for the City building contract that my sickly father and I had won to build a new street linking the Waverley Station with the High Street, a street which would later be named Cockburn Street, it made sense to employ him – I needed grafters, he needed a job. The job, and my friendship with Michael, or Mick as everyone called him, would eventually lead me on a fantastic adventure.

My name is Jim, or Jimmy, Reid, and I was born and grew up in Edinburgh. My father, James, was a builder to trade, but his poor health and advancing years of 50 had curtailed his involvement in the building trade, leaving me to run our wee squad myself. I served my time as a stonemason but could turn my hand to almost anything – which was just as well, as most masonry jobs were given to 'favoured men' among Edinburgh's elite.

My older brother Davie had been killed fighting in the British Army in 1855 during The Crimean War.

He had died, not from a Cossack's blade nor a Russian bullet, but of typhus, a horrible disease with no known cure. He wasn't alone – for every ten soldiers that the British Army lost in the Crimea, only one died from actual combat. We had heard that he had distinguished himself in some minor engagements, but that mattered little – he was gone and that's just the way it is. As well as our little building squad, we had a small Ironmonger's shop about halfway down the High Street, and I lived in the little flat above the shop with my mother,

Mary, and my father. They ran the shop, I ran the building squad. We were by no means wealthy, but we survived.

Though my mother, father and I were Protestants, we were Episcopalian rather than Presbyterian, so that always made doing business in Edinburgh a little bit difficult. Some Scots saw Episcopalianism as a form of diluted Catholicism, but most in Edinburgh simply didn't know what being Episcopalian meant, though they knew that we attended different services to most of them. I always found the Scottish obsession with religion to be an embarrassing relic of our troubled past. I counted men from all three faiths as my friends, and was proud to do so. Popular prejudice at the time in Edinburgh painted the Irish in the Cowgate as some sort of fifth column, here in Edinburgh to steal our jobs and subvert 'our' religion. Through Mick and my other Irish friends, I saw that this simply wasn't the case. The immigrants were here to save, and hopefully improve, their lives, as all people deserve the chance to do so. I despaired at some of the Anti-Irish rhetoric used by everyone from Presbyterian ministers to drunks in the High Street's taverns. There were two main reasons for this despair. My father always taught me to never judge men by the group, to take men 'one at a time', as he put it. Moreover, I found the bigotry of a minority of the Presbyterians to be completely hypocritical – they were taught, as we were, to love their neighbour and not to judge others, yet those two lessons were conveniently forgotten whenever they saw fit. As I say that, I should point out that Edinburgh was a fairly cosmopolitan city in those days, and most people's chief concern was making a living rather than being righteous- as the drunkenness and whoring that engulfed the city of an evening back then plainly showed. However, sometimes religion did matter when it came to finding and keeping work, as we were to find out, in the most cruel way.

Chapter Four - The New Job

Our trouble began when we started work on that new street which the council wanted built to connect the railway station with the High Street. I had a five man squad, myself, three regulars from Edinburgh, and Mick. On the first day of the job we realised that every building squad in Edinburgh had been enlisted to help with the project – that was fine- but we also learned that overall stewardship of the project had been given to a man called Ebenezer Ogilvie, a vile, corrupt but well-connected fat bigoted man in his mid fifties. He owned the most successful Ironmonger's in the High Street – it always undercut ours- and he also owned the Tolbooth Inn in the Canongate, a popular but decidedly dodgy establishment which also served as the headquarters of his family businesses. Wherever Ebenezer went, his two vile sons also went, to act as his bodyguards and as his tools for intimidating Edinburgh's people. The brothers were a little bit older than me, in fact, years earlier they had beaten up my own brother over a supposed gambling debt and even tried to threaten my father into closing down the shop.

They only backed off when we managed to corner them one night while I was with some men from our building squad- there was no fight, but our show of strength deterred Ogilvie from any further attempts to put us out of business, at least temporarily.

My family and our employees rarely drank in Ogilvie's inn – we drank in The Clachan, a smaller, more friendly inn which was next door to our shop. That's the inn where Mick first saw our 'help wanted' sign. The Clachan was owned by a widower named Hume, who was as honest as the day is long, and was a close family friend.

Ogilvie and his sons may have been nasty pieces of work, but Margaret, the youngest of their family, a bonnie lass with long dark brown hair, alluring brown eyes and a shapely but womanly physique, was a different kettle of fish. I had known her almost all of my life, admiring her from afar. She worked in her father's inn, and was the only girl who worked there who didn't offer to sell customers her body as well as food and drink. She was off limits. She was beautiful- and seemed a nice lassie, different, but she was

13

Ogilvie's property, and would probably be married off to one of his business associates as a 'sweetener' at some time when it suited Ogilvie. Whenever I saw Margaret in the High Street or on the odd occasion that I did visit the Tolbooth Inn, I got the feeling that she liked me, but there our 'relationship' stalled – social convention and local politics making her unattainable to me.

Our trouble with Ebenezer Ogilvie began two weeks into the building job. He appeared on the site one Tuesday morning in his tall hat and heavily starched suit and waistcoat, flanked as ever by his two gruesome sons. He called a halt to our work and stood on a soap-box while his sons summoned each squad to come and listen to him. His news startled us all.

'Now listen here men, I've got some bad news from yesterday's council meeting that concerns us all. The town council have forced me to cut some costs on this job. I can't cut capital costs, so it must be labour. What shall I do? Shall I lay men off?'

This statement was greeted with unanimous growls of 'no' from the assembled squads that made up his workforce. He continued.

'Right then, it seems fairer to me that all should have less than some should have none. Wages will be cut by one quarter for all junior foremen and labourers alike .And we will also have to wait until next month to be paid. We all have to tighten our belts.'

'I don't see your belt getting any tighter, Mr. Ogilvie' replied Tam Brodie, one of my fellow squad leaders, pointing at Ogilvie's obscenely swollen fat stomach. Ogilvie was quick to respond.

'In that case Brodie, you and your squad won't be needed tomorrow, take what tools are yours and go home. Maybe that'll teach you to respect your betters.'

Wee Tam looked at his startled men, looked at his feet for a moment, then sheepishly responded.

'No Mr. Ogilvie sir, that won't be necessary. We can do the job'.

'Fair enough' grunted Ogilvie, secretly pleased that he wasn't losing a squad but appearing to be being magnanimous about the whole affair.

I was enraged. But what was to come next made me even angrier. Ogilvie continued.

'Oh, and wages for immigrant workers will be cut by a third. In these tough times, we need to make sure that real Edinburgh men are looked after first. Immigrant workers are welcome to continue working, at the new reduced rate. If anyone doesn't like it, there are hundreds of men in Edinburgh who will be willing to take their place, so, make the best of it and knuckle-down, and pray our budget is cut no further'.

And with that, the fat, red-faced monster stepped down from his soap-box and started walking away, with his sons, as if he had only dropped in to bid us good day, rather than to ruin our livelihoods.

All the men just stood there, stunned. The wages on this job were low enough as it was without being cut! Now what were they supposed to do?

I wasn't thinking about myself, but of my men, especially Mick – how would he manage with such a pay cut? He could barely manage as things were. I ran after Ogilvie, in a desperate attempt to have him reconsider. He doffed his hat to me, and seemed willing to listen while we were out of earshot of the others. I spoke politely but firmly.

'Mr. Ogilvie, my squad have been doing most of the digging, by far the hardest part of this job, and my best worker is an Irishman. Please sir, reconsider this decision, I implore you. You can even take from my own pay to give to Mick if needs be.'

Ogilvie scoffed 'Oh Mick's your Irishman is he? You really should be more careful about who you choose to employ, young Reid. And as for the wages, that's a point of principle – I'm not taking pay from a reasonably good Scots foreman like you to give to some unskilled potato-famine bog trotter like him, and if I find out that you or any of your other boys have been subsidising him, and I WILL find out, your whole squad's off the job, do you understand me?'

'Even though he's the best worker in my squad, in any of the squads, come to think of it?' I said.

'Not even if he built the whole bloody street himself. Now, get back to work, in any case, all this is out of my hands, I can't help it if the council cuts the budget. Good day to you, young Reid' said

Ogilvie, as he turned and waddled off after his two sons, both of whom had watched our entire conversation.

I returned to my sullen squad. They said nothing – they knew it wasn't my fault, but that didn't make me, or them, feel any better. We worked as long as there was daylight, then I bought my squad a drink in The Clachan afterwards. It's amazing what some ale and banter can do to make people forget about a bad situation, at least temporarily. As my other three squad men, Smith, Grant and Munro, said good night and went home to their lodgings, I at last had the chance to talk to Mick about his victimisation by Ogilvie. I did my best to explain, but Mick was very calm, and spoke.

'Listen now Jim, you don't need to apologise, it's not your fault, and do you know, the funny thing is, that fat bastard Ogilvie is my landlord in the Cowgate. As soon as I saw him on site I knew there would be trouble. He recently laid-off the man whose family I lodge with, even though he's his tenant. They owe him a month's rent. Next week it'll be two. I left Ireland to get away from fat greedy landlords like that, I never once thought you'd have them here as well. Must be the way of the world'.

We had another drink together, then we went our separate ways for the evening. Two things happened that night that were to change everything.

Chapter Five – From Bad To Worse

Mick got home to the Cowgate to find that the family that he had lodged with had been murdered.

City Police were on the scene and allowed Mick into the little 'home' to see what had happened. At first Mick was relieved that the officers present didn't think that he had anything to do with the murder, but the reason for this became all too apparent to Mick as he saw the gruesome spectacle in the house.

Mrs. McCredie and her two small children had all died from slit throats, while Mr. McCredie was found with slit wrists, a cut throat AND a huge blood-stained razor in his hand. Mick knew straight away what had happened.

One of the policemen was clearly upset by the bodies, the blood, and the very nature of the crime, exclaiming 'he must have gone temporarily insane', as the other officers agreed. Mick knew different. Mr. McCredie was nearly two months behind with the rent, he had no job, he had two young children and a wife to provide for, and no social safety net of either an extended family nearby or help from the council. As there was every possibility that the repugnant Mr. Ogilvie had told all his business chums not to employ Mr. McCredie, the poor man had seen a future so dark for him and his family that death was the only escape from it. Some would say that he had indeed gone temporarily insane, but Mick also saw the other viewpoint – to keep them alive in a state of perpetual poverty sounded like permanent insanity. Mick wished that they had asked him to contribute more rent, he wished they had told him about their plight, but they had been proud people. There was nothing Mick could do except retrieve what few belongings he had from his lodging room, and never return to the tenement. Late that night he appeared at our door, just after the second thing had happened.

That second thing to happen that night was a conversation that I had with my Father, not long before a shocked Mick appeared at our home with news of the heartbreaking crime. I told Father about Ogilvie's news about our wages and the cuts to them, and about

Ogilvie's bigoted attitude towards Mick. I was astounded by Father's response. He spoke at length.

'Son, that Ogilvie bastard came into the shop with his sons today. He tried to bully me into selling the shop to him at a knockdown rate, and threatened that no-one in town would buy goods from us if we didn't. When I refused, he implied that we may be robbed, or suffer a fire.'

'What did you do?' I asked angrily.

'I told him to go to the devil! It'll take more than threats from him to make me give up our livelihood. He's been at Mr. Hume to sell him The Clachan too, with the same sales pitch no doubt. Mr. Hume refused him as well.'

I was doubly infuriated. I asked Father what could be done.

'Not a lot son. Ogilvie practically owns the High Street. He's no just a businessman, Son, he's a pimp, a thief, a bully, a bigot and a gang master. Because he indirectly owns most of the taverns around here, and controls most of the whores and toughs, he knows everybody's secrets, and those whose secrets he doesn't know, he can easily threaten or bribe to stay out of his way. Nearly everybody's in his pocket, even the council and the police – and no-one in authority wants him removed, either because they don't want things he knows about them to become public, or because they don't want gang warfare on the streets between his minions should anything happen to him – he'd leave quite a big power vacuum, do you see, Son?'.

'Aye, Da' I said. Father continued.

'I'll tell you one thing though, I know all about his 'budget cut' from the council and guilds for that street you're building- it's pure fantasy. What's actually happened is that he's been offered a big bonus if he completes the new street on time, so his greed has dictated that he'll double that bonus by cutting his workers' wages – pure greed son.'

'So how did you get rid of him earlier, Father?' I asked, assuming that he hadn't taken Father's rejection gracefully.

'Well son, that was easy. He thought those two big oafish sons of his would intimidate me, but I reminded him that I have you, and your squad, and that even powerful greedy men like him should sleep with one eye open. I then pulled out the pistol from under the counter and politely asked him to leave, so he did.'

'He'll be raging' I said.

'Hopefully, yes he will be' said Father, smiling. 'He won't come back round here anyway. Remember, Son, your brother was a war-hero and we're a respectable, honourable family. That still counts for something in this 'toon. Not a lot, but enough to deter scum like Ogilvie from doing anything illegal.'

It was then that Mick arrived at our house with his new tale of woe. We ate together and talked for a while. Father and I were shocked but not surprised at Ogilvie's indirect involvement in the murder of that Irish family, but Father saw it differently to how Mick and I did. Father was confident that Ogilvie could and should just be ignored. Mick and I were angry to the extreme- the wages, that family, the threats to my Father, and with the intemperance of youth, both of us thought that something should be done about him. We both went to work the next day normally, we worked until it was too dark to continue doing so, just like normal, but what we did next was far from normal. We went back to the family Ironmonger's and 'borrowed' two long, thin steel knives. Then we marched straight down the High Street towards the Tolbooth Inn, Ebenezer Ogilvie's inn...

Chapter Six – Unexpected Delights

As Jim and Mick walked down the cobbled High Street, their long knives discretely hidden in their clothes, and the occasional chamber pot's contents narrowly missing their heads as the human waste splattered to the ground from the upper tenements, always with a useless warning cry of 'Garde de l'eau', they talked about what they were going to do. Jim spoke.

'Listen Mick, I really appreciate your help and you coming with me here, Christ there's no-one I'd rather have watching my back at a time like this, but this will get nasty – presently you're not involved – wouldn't you rather keep it that way?'

'I AM involved Jimmy lad, this Ogilvie cut my wages and caused the death of my landlord, and he's insulted you my friend, and your family. I'm coming. I've dealt with bastards like this before back in Ireland, except this time I can...' he paused.

'You can what?' asked Jim.

'I can make a better show of things than I did the last time, that's what I can do – is this the place?' asked Mick as they reached The Tolbooth Inn.

'Aye' said Jim.

'Then let's do this' said Mick, his voice full of confidence.

Both men walked through the creaking door of the Inn, ready to pounce upon Ebenezer Ogilvie, and his two sons, and any of his other toughs who might be hanging around the Inn. It was time for retribution.

Though late in the evening, the tobacco smoke-filled main room was relatively empty – it was midweek after all. There was a crude bar in one corner near the smaller back entrance, there were six big Oak tables that dominated the downstairs layout, and a small winding staircase lead up to what were euphemistically called 'the lodging rooms'. The lodging rooms were supposed to be for travellers who were staying at the Inn, but everybody in Edinburgh knew that they were where Ogilvie's serving-girls come- prostitutes took their customers to ply their trade. A warm, hearty fire burned in the fireplace, and that, with the smell of ale and tobacco, gave the establishment a warm, if slightly smelly, atmosphere.

Jim and Mick looked around. There was no sign of Ogilvie, or of his sons, nor indeed of any of their heavies. There were four very inebriated men sitting at two of the tables, slugging ale as they ogled the more than ample charms of the 'serving girls' who milled around them. Unsure what to do next, the two men sat down at one of the empty tables. As soon as they sat down, they were approached by a girl in a long, well-worn white dress. Her hair was covered by the sort of headscarf-come-hood that was attached to most women's' dresses, but that did nothing to hide her charm.

She had big, beautiful brown eyes and an unmistakably feminine curvy figure; even her ankle length dress couldn't hide that. A few strands of dark-brown hair hung down from her odd headgear, but even then, she was by far the most beautiful of all the serving-girls in the Inn. It was Margaret, Ogilvie's young daughter, and she appeared to be running the Inn herself on this particular evening. Without being asked, she brought over two huge wooden mugs of ale for Mick and Jim, and a smaller mug for herself, and she sat down beside them and spoke. Jim could hardly take his eyes off her.

'Well if it isn't wee Jimmy Reid! That young laddie who used to stare at me all the time! I never expected to see you in here again – but it's good to see you Jimmy- and who's your friend?'

Jim was at first un-nerved by her friendliness and familiarity, but he introduced Mick to Margaret and Margaret seemed pleased to meet him. Margaret took a big gulp from her mug of ale, then spoke again.

'So, what brings you two laddies in here this evening? If you're looking for my father I'm afraid you've had a wasted journey – he's in West Lothian with my brothers, Silas and George, and the rest of the boys – trouble with a tenant in Broxburn I think. Some wee farmer who won't sell his farm to make way for a mine. They'll no be back 'till the 'morn.'

Jim quickly decided that it would perhaps be a tad imprudent to tell Margaret that he and his Irish friend had come to the Inn to tear her Father and Brothers and anyone else who got in their way to bloody rags, so, in a rare move, he lied.

'Ach Margaret we got sick of The Clachan and the same auld songs, so we decided to come here for a change. I do want to speak to Mr. Ogilvie about a business matter but that can wait – we're just here to have a bit of fun tonight- aren't we Mick?'

'Um, yeah' answered Mick, unsure what Jim was doing but doing his best to play along. Not that there seemed anything to worry about – the atmosphere in the unusually quiet Inn gave him no cause to worry. 'Just a bit of ale and fun' Mick added.

Jim couldn't take his eyes off Margaret, though completely clothed he could see that her breasts were straining to be released from her long dress, and every time she spoke she transfixed him with her eyes and voice. Margaret then spoke.

'So what's it to be, boys? More ale? Some food? Or some REAL fun?' She winked as she said the last part of her question.

'What's real fun?' asked Mick.

Margaret shouted to one of the other serving girls, a blonde girl in her mid 20's with deep -set blue eyes and whose enormous breasts were practically bursting out of her dress.

'This is Jane, say hello to Mick and Jimmy, Jane' said Margaret.

'Hello boys' said Jane. Noticing Mick's red-hair, Jane spoke some more.

'So you're that handsome Irishman everyone's been talking about, are you Mick? More ale?'

Before any of the three at the table could answer, Jane was off getting another big tankard of ale, which she duly placed on the table, before sitting directly opposite Mick. The four of them began to drink.

And drink.

After an hour or so, the rest of the male drinkers had left, and after clearing up, Margaret told the other girls to go home, leaving Mick, Jim, her and Jane alone in the Inn. Soon Jim and Mick had forgotten about their original reason for visiting the Tolbooth Inn, and were laughing and talking with the girls. Mick's Irish charm wasn't wasted on Jane, who was constantly stroking his red hair and touching his arm as they talked, Mick was transfixed by her as he drank more, no doubt his ardour heated by the sight of her deep cleavage only a foot or so from his face as they talked and laughed.

Jim wasn't so flirtatious with Margaret, he knew that he was walking on eggshells whether her father was there or not – but he wanted her, and now he was as close to her as he had ever been. As the ale flowed and the evening wore on, eventually Jane whispered something to Mick, who smiled and nodded, before Jane took him by the hand and led him up the stairs towards one of the lodging rooms. Jane shouted down the stairs 'never had an Irish one before, Miss Margaret, first time for everything!'

'You be gentle with him now' shouted Margaret back at her, before she turned to Jim and spoke.

'I'm disappointed Jimmy, I thought you and your friend had come here to sort out that horrible father of mine. I mean, I wouldn't blame you after everything he's done.'

Jim was flabbergasted at her perception, but kept his cool, and her beauty and apparent honesty forced him to lie again.

'No, we didn't come here to deprive you of any family members, Margaret' he said, hoping that would be an end to the matter.

'That's a pity, I was really hoping that you would' said Margaret , as she glugged yet more ale then smiled at Jim, catching his gaze and holding it, looking deep into his eyes before speaking again.

'I hate him, and my brothers, and all their vile friends. They have the run of the city, they do whatever they want – but me, I'm forced to run this glorified brothel for them, yet they expect me to live like a nun. '

'What do you mean?' asked Jim.

'I run this bloody place for them, deal with all the customers, handle the girls, but I get no thanks. And as for the men-'

Jim interrupted. 'I thought you weren't like the other girls Margaret, you don't go upstairs with customers, do you?'

'Jesus, no' said Margaret. 'If any man even asks, my father and brothers will throw them off The Crags! No, I meant that I'm not allowed to court or see any men. Father says he's waiting for the right man to match me up with, but I know what that'll involve. I'm 21 years old, like you, I want to be married, but not to one of Father's grotesque old cronies, I don't want some fat ugly old man grunting and sweating all over me then expecting me to clean his house and raise his children, just because it suits my family - I want to love, love a man of my own choosing'. She emptied her mug of ale and then refilled it again, topping up Jim's as she did so.

Jim was no expert with women, but he could tell that she wanted him, and he wanted to help her to escape, so he listened, and drank.

'It's not just this place Jimmy, when we're at home Father often beats me. He even lets Silas and George watch sometimes, he says it's so that they know how to treat their own wives, if they ever find any.'

Jim was disgusted by this revelation, how could anyone mistreat such a pretty young woman? He spoke.

'Have you ever thought about running away?'

'Where would I go? They don't let me have much money, and no-one at the railway station or the port in Leith would let me on a ship or a train alone – they'd be signing their own death warrant. I'm stuck here'.

Jim thought about what she had just said. She was right. Ogilvie's combined contacts and associates in the council, The Masons, The Protestant Society, and in most of Edinburgh's commerce and trade institutions made it unlikely that she would escape successfully. She sounded genuine, so he bit the bullet and spoke.

'Margaret dear, you know I've always admired you from afar, don't you?'

'Even when you put that big spider in my hair when we were bairns?'

'Aye, even then' laughed Jim.

'What if you were free from your Father and brothers, what then?' he asked.

'What do you mean?' she asked.

A little the worse for wear from drink, and against his better judgement, Jim pulled his knife from his belt to show her, then he placed it on the empty chair that had been vacated by Mick.

Margaret looked shocked, but not disgusted, and asked Jim to explain himself.

'Well, Margaret, what if your Father and brothers were never to return from West Lothian? What if five armed men jumped on them out at Newbridge tomorrow and killed them all before they got home? Or even if they just killed Mr. Ogilvie and made sure your brothers knew not to return to Edinburgh-'

Jim stopped. Had he gone too far? He hoped not. Margaret's response shocked him.

'My Father killed my mother, you know that don't you? I think that's a braw idea – but you'll need more than knives, and who are your other men?'

Jim continued. 'My building squad, Smith, Grant and Munro, and Mick of course. My father has plenty of guns. No-one need ever know what happened to them, and then you'd be free.'

Margaret was quiet for a moment, and then spoke.

'You mean Mick who is upstairs with Jane, well he certainly sounds strong enough doesn't he?' Margaret was referring to Jane's screams of orgasmic delight emanating from upstairs, a noise that Margaret and Jim had managed to ignore until then, even when Mick let out periodic Wolf-like howls.

They both laughed, drunk but still able to speak. Margaret then lowered her tone of voice and spoke.

'Jimmy, I know it's wrong, but what they do to me is wrong, and I know you're itching for a showdown with them anyway, shall you do it then?'

Jim was relieved. The sin of murder that he was going to commit would be off-set by helping free Margaret from her awful family situation.

'Aye Margaret, I will, or rather, my friends and I will'.

Margaret burst into tears and then threw her arms around him, kissing him on the cheek.

'How can I ever repay you?' she said to Jim as she dried her tears.

Jim ducked out of making the obvious comment, and instead said 'ridding Edinburgh of Mr. Ogilvie is reward enough, we aren't just doing this for you, but, since you asked...'

They were interrupted by a half-dressed Mick clumping down the stairs, hurriedly re-dressing himself.

Jim spoke.

'Listen, Mick, I need you to go and see Smith, Grant and Munro, tell them it's important and to meet at The Ironmonger's shop tomorrow at eight o'clock sharp- they'll know what it's about.'

Mick casually asked 'are you sure you'll be alright here Jim lad?'

Jim and Margaret looked at each other, then Jim said 'aye, please do it now Mick, I'll be home soon, oh and try not to wake my parents when you go to sleep at our house'.

He winked at Mick, who winked back, turned, and then turned again to reply to both of them.

'Now that was some ride! Like Helen of Troy with her arse on fire!'

All three of them laughed, and then Mick was gone, out into Edinburgh's dark night. Jane came down the stairs a few moments later. She was dressed again but her hair was now a complete mess.

'Well, what was he like?' asked Margaret.

'Oh he was like a bloody Bull, he was so good that I forgot to charge him!'

All three of them laughed, before Jane asked Margaret if she could finish for the night, and as it was a bit late, she asked to sleep upstairs, which Margaret agreed to. She said goodnight and went upstairs to bed, leaving Jim and Margaret alone again.

'Now, where were we?' said Margaret as she double-locked the Inn's heavy door. 'Oh yes I remember, how am I going to repay you for rescuing me?'

'No payment is necessary, Margaret, honestly. We were going to kill him anyway.'

'No, not payment, but I want to show my appreciation' she said.

Jim knew what was coming next, or at least, he thought he knew. Margaret was full of surprises.

Margaret was still standing up and then she suddenly turned around and lifted up the back of her long dress and skirts, showing her shapely legs and curvaceous posterior to Jim, slapping her own backside and groping it, wiggling her hips slightly, her hands on another table as she bent over more.

'Do you like what you see, Jim? Does this please you?' she asked.

Before Jim could answer, she had turned around and was walking towards him, unbuttoning her dress so that her firm cleavage was on display. Jim was transfixed.

'Only one man's ever had his hands on my body, Jim, and he's at the bottom of The Forth after Father found out. Would you like to put your hands all over me?'

Something inside Jim told him that this situation would somehow end badly, but the ale and his lust for Margaret clouded his judgement. He didn't lift his hands to touch her, even when she stood right in front of him, kissed him passionately, and then pulled his face into her cleavage. Jim was in seventh heaven as he kissed her breasts and heard her moan gently, but he decided no, this was as far as things would go. Then, within a flash it seemed, Margaret was completely naked in front of him, apart from her puritan-esque headgear.

'Are you a shy boy, Jim? Are you a virgin?' she giggled.

Before Jim could answer, Margaret had whipped away her headgear, and her long beautiful brown hair spilled down almost all of the way down to her hips, partially covering her heaving breasts, her beautiful brown eyes blazing with lust.

Jim could take no more, and swept her into his arms. She whispered to him 'I've always wanted you, and now you're mine' as they kissed again, and then she kissed his neck, and soon the couple were having sex on one of the big oak tables, and then over one of them, and then with Jim in a chair while Margaret straddled him. She felt so good to him. Jim used all his self-control not to risk making her pregnant, but her strokes felt so good as she bounced up and down in his lap. She started to scream and moan in delight, and Jim felt her wetness contracting around his manhood as she orgasmed, Margaret scratching his back and neck and biting hard on his lip , making it bleed, before she started urging him to 'whip his cream', which he soon did. She collapsed into his arms, both of them sweaty, both exhausted, after a good hour's lovemaking.

'Shall we go upstairs to bed?' asked Margaret, already knowing what the answer would be.

'Aye, lets' said Jim, and soon the two lovers were entwined together upstairs in bed, where they fell asleep in each other's arms. Margaret clung to Jim all night as if she had been shipwrecked and he was the last piece of floating wreckage. Jim couldn't believe how the evening had turned out. He had watched Margaret from afar and now he had had her, with the added bonus of knowing how livid her father and brothers would be when they found out. If they found out. Jim enjoyed a blissful night of deep, virtuous sleep.

Chapter Seven – Rude Awakenings

I woke the next morning in a strange bed, but soon remembered where I was. It was still early, and she was still next to me, asleep. I couldn't believe what had happened last night. My early morning joy was somewhat tempered when I remembered that I had a rather gruesome day ahead, in which I would probably have to kill at least one man, albeit an evil one, in order to uphold my family's honour , save a damsel in distress and also rid Edinburgh of a man who was its scourge. That was the plan, until Silas and George Ogilvie burst through the bedroom door carrying pistols. They told me not to move, and then motioned their sister to get out of bed before telling her 'downstairs now'. She got out of bed and did so coolly and unquestioningly, not even being given time to dress herself and without so much as a glance at me. I reached for my breaches in an attempt to retrieve my knife from its belt, but was told 'Don't try it' by Silas, as both men dragged me out of the room naked and marched me downstairs. There I saw Margaret again, wrapped in a blanket, avoiding eye contact with me. It was then that I realised that I had been tricked!

Then I saw a fat older man in a tall hat sitting beside the fireplace. He was laughing, which made his sons laugh too. They were laughing at me. I then remembered that I had left my knife on a chair downstairs, but when I looked at the chairs it was nowhere to be seen. Ebenezer Ogilvie had me exactly where he wanted me.

At first his attention wasn't focused on me, he got out of his chair and strode over to where Margaret was still shivering under a blanket, avoiding eye contact with everyone – she looked just as scared as me.

'You little whore! You were supposed to drug the wretch then keep him here until this morning, not bed the bastard! You little whore!' He slapped her face, twice, hard, and she wept as he continued to call her degrading names. Oddly, at this moment I found myself agreeing in my head with everything he said to her, but I wasn't going to join in. Ogilvie then sent her upstairs to get dressed and told her to go and wake Jane, and off she went upstairs. Then he turned his attention to me.

'So, wee Jimmy, you and your Irish friend and that squad of yours were going to jump on us this morning were you? Going to kill me and my boys were you? Well I've got news for you, son. Your friends Smith, Grant and Munro are gone for good. Some of my men went round to their lodgings this morning and rounded them up, we put them on the first boat out of Leith, Christ knows where they're going, but they won't be coming back to Edinburgh. They're lucky I didn't kill them'

I asked him if he was going to kill me. Oddly, he replied that he hadn't decided yet. Then we heard a blood-curdling scream from upstairs. It was Margaret screaming, and though her distress now sounded like music to my ears, I did wonder what was going on. As I stood there shivering and naked in front of these three brutes, I thought that my time had come. 'George' growled Ogilvie to his other son, who went upstairs without asking what he was supposed to do, which made me nervous.

I still had Silas's pistol pointed at me though, so even though the numerical odds against me had improved, my prospects for survival really hadn't. George re-appeared at the top of the stairs and threw my clothes at me. I needed no invitation to get dressed. Margaret was wailing and crying upstairs, until her father shouted 'shut that blubbing up, lassie, unless you want to join her!'

As I finished dressing, still with a loaded pistol pointed at me, I saw what the screaming was all about. George carried a blood-soaked dead woman in his arms. It was Jane, the serving girl who Mick had only last night been coupling with. Her throat had been cut and she had multiple other injuries of a slashing nature. Ogilvie told George to lay her down on the table in front of me, which he did, before re-pointing his own pistol at me.

'What happened to that poor lassie?' I asked aloud.

Ogilvie replied that he was hoping I would be able to tell him that. I didn't say anything else, I already suspected the worst, before Ogilvie finally spoke again, as he puffed on a cigar.

'It's perfectly obvious what's happened here, Reid. You plotted to kill me and my boys, but when you got here you found only women, including my defenceless wee daughter. You rode one of my serving girls, then you refused to pay her, you argued over it, so you sliced her up good style with this knife'.

To my horror, Ogilvie held up the long thin blade that I had taken from our family shop, the one that I had left on the chair the previous evening, and it was indeed covered in blood. I was terrified, but Ogilvie had more to say.

'And then, to make it even worse, you attacked and raped my own wee beloved daughter in my own establishment when she tried to challenge you. It's common knowledge that you've always had your eye on her. So that's a murder and a rape in one night, no bad going Jimmy boy, you're a man after my own heart' he sneered, as his sons laughed, their pistols still levelled at me.

'You know that's not what happened, Mr. Ogilvie' I said, simply but firmly, but it was no use. He continued.

'Oh I know that. See, I knew that you and that taig companion of yours would come after me the very next day after I went to see your dear Father about selling me his shop. Why do you think I went to see him and behaved like that? And you took the bait, you did exactly what I knew you would do. And then you fell for the oldest trick in the book, my daughter and her quim brought you to this end, laddie.

It's much easier to catch a man when his breaches are down. And then there's this knife, covered in blood, and only one ironmonger in Edinburgh sells this type of knife, and it's not me, it's YOU, and your family. I even know that your pathetic Father hasn't even sold any of these knives yet, so if the city police were to check his inventory and ledgers at his shop, they'd know the murder weapon came from you. And then, of course, there's three witnesses, me and my two sons, who came back in the nick of time and stopped you right in the middle of raping our Margaret. You're covered in bite marks and scratches, how else did you get them? And all those bruises.'

He turned to Margaret who had dressed and come downstairs while he was speaking, but she still avoided eye contact with me. 'At least you were finally useful for something ya wee whore' he sneered. She just stared at the ground.

31

I instinctively asked 'what bruises?' , so Ogilvie nodded towards me and then his two huge sons handed him their pistols and then proceeded to beat me near senseless. I thumped George on the nose but soon realised that this was all part of their plan. When they stopped beating me, I pulled myself up so that I was sitting at the table. The brothers re-armed themselves with the pistols. My mouth was full of blood.

'Father, that's enough, please, don't hurt him anymore' I heard Margaret tearfully say, but a slap on the jaw from Silas soon shut her up. It was then that I decided that I was going to die, so I had nothing to lose – I asked.

'So Mr. Ogilvie, what is it that you want? Clearly you don't just want to kill me, or else why go to such elaborate lengths to set me up like this? You know no-one in the city-clique will believe me over you, and even if they did they wouldn't dare say it aloud. So, Mr. Ogilvie, tell me what it is you want'.

He paused for a moment, put out his cigar, then spoke.

'It's perfectly simple Jimmy. There's only going to be one Ironmonger in the High Street, and that's me. There's only going to be one builder, and that's me, and there's going to be no Irish, Catholics or Episcopalians working on my sites. I want your family's shop, the house above it, all the stock, even the clothes off your back. In short, I want you all out of Edinburgh, and you'll sign everything your family has over to me, for nothing. If you don't, then I call in the City Police, you get hanged for murder and rape, and no-one will ever do business with your family again, so they'll lose everything anyway – but with you gone and your dead brother worm food in The Crimea, who's going to look after your mother and father? It can be a dangerous, nasty world, Reid. If everything is signed over to me, we'll forget all about this nasty incident, Silas and George will dump wee Jane here in The Forth, you and your family can leave town in peace, and your wee attack on my daughter and your conspiracy to murder never happened.

By the way, we were next door all night, we gave it half an hour after he heard you and my daughter finally give it a rest in the bedroom, then George here sneaked in and cut up wee Jane'. George smiled at this, then Ogilvie simply said 'what's it to be then?'

I knew that they had me. They had caught me using the oldest trick in the book, my anger and my lust had done the rest. I had no choice but to agree, but, even from my weakened position, I tried to add a caveat by asking one question – what had happened to Mick?

To my surprise, Ogilvie answered my question. He said he didn't know, but he let me in on a secret.

His 'boys' – which could have meant his sons or his henchmen-had found out from a drunken sailor in Leith that Mick was a wanted man in Ireland for shooting and killing his landlord. Mick's presence in Edinburgh had been brought to the attention of the city police and Mick knew it, so he had done a bunk.

I was deflated. Mick could have been my witness if I had reneged on the deal and fought the case in court, not that a Scottish court would have taken the testimony of an Irishman already wanted for murder as gospel. Ogilvie then told me to go 'up the road' and get the deeds for our shop and home, Silas was to accompany me, in case I tried to abscond – not that I could really do that anyway, Ogilvie's plot had already seen to that. I made my way towards the door.

BANG. THUMP.

The gun going off startled everyone in the room, except George Ogilvie, whose head it had blown apart, sending the body thumping to the wooden floor. Margaret let out a scream as his blood and brains splattered over her face, and I turned to see Mick coming in the other door, with a smoking flintlock pistol in his hand. He then dropped the pistol and pulled his knife. Silas Ogilvie didn't know who to shoot, and his moment's hesitation was his downfall. He aimed at my belly and fired his pistol, just as his sister Margaret whacked him on the back of the head with a stool. The shot missed, ricocheting noisily around the room. Silas went for his blade but before he could draw it, Mick was upon him, beating him savagely with his fists. It turned out that Big Silas was no match for an angry Irishman, and Silas was soon still.

As Mick was beating Silas, I rushed towards Ogilvie himself, who had pulled a tiny two-shot pistol from his coat. I kicked it out of his hand before he could even cock it, and then I kicked him in the teeth. He fell to the floor, so I put my foot on his neck and bent down to pick up his little ladies' gun. Mick closed the door, then gasped in horror as he saw Jane's mutilated corpse. Mick seemed to know that Margaret had set us up but I asked him not to hurt her, so he didn't. I saw a solitary tear run down his face as he looked down at the sliced up corpse who only last night had taken his virginity. We were now in almost as difficult a position as we had been before Mick burst in. George was dead, Silas was dying, and we had that fat old bigoted bastard Ogilvie at our mercy. We also had to decide what to do about Margaret.

I then did something that I think will haunt me forever. Remembering Ogilvie saying that he even wanted the clothes of my family's backs, I took one of my socks and stuffed it into his mouth, right down his throat, and then I held his nose. He struggled and struggled, turning blue, gasping, and I think the last words that he ever heard anyone say were from me.

'Well Mr. Ogilvie, there's only one Ironmonger in Edinburgh's High Street now, and there, can you taste my clothes, how does it feel, fat-man?'

I eventually put the horrible fat man out of his misery by stamping on his neck. With one crack, he was still, and he and both of his sons were dead.

'Jim, I don't want to add more pressure to the situation but we'd better be getting the hell out of here' said Mick. 'But what do we do with her?' He pointed at Margaret, who had cleaned the brains and blood from her face and was just sitting staring into space.

I remembered the wondrous night that I had spent with her, and in the same instant remembered the position that being seduced by her and her friend had put Mick and I in. At least the other boys had gotten away so there was no-one to back up the 'conspiracy to murder' story. Part of me wanted to shoot her, but she had also saved us at a vital moment by striking her own brother. It was only a matter of time before the police would arrive to investigate the gunshots, so, oddly, Margaret had to decide what we did next. I didn't think it wise to drag her along with us against her will, as given that we had just killed her whole family I suspected that that might make her just a tad peevish. On the other hand, we couldn't just leave her there to tell the police what had happened. So, I asked her what she wanted to do.

'We get the hell out of here, today. There are about 200 gold sovereigns in a sack behind the bar, and Father and my brothers will be carrying money'.

Mick and I soon relieved the three corpses of their money, while Margaret grabbed the sovereigns.

And then we set the Inn on fire.

It was the only way to hide the events. We started a small fire - which took about an hour to become noticeable- and then locked the doors and left, carrying nothing but the money and the clothes we stood in. We walked up the High Street to my family's shop. I'm ashamed to say that I left without saying goodbye to my parents, but I did give a young lad two sovereigns to run into the shop and hand a sack to my father containing 100 of the sovereigns. And so we, this curious trio, made our way to Princes Street and boarded a train that would take us from Edinburgh, to Carstairs, then Glasgow, and finally, to London. As luck would have it, we were out of Edinburgh by the time the fire in the Tolbooth Inn was even noticed. The three of us didn't say much on the 18 hour train journey south – so long because we had to change at several stations along the way. Eventually, the three of us got to London. Whether we liked it or not, we were now bonded by those crazy events in Edinburgh. Myself, I felt dishonoured, cowardly, and fearful. I had committed murder – albeit in self-defence- and fled the scene like a dishonourable coward. None of us could go back to Scotland for a long time - that was for sure.

We rented rooms at a cheap, dirty hotel in London for a few nights while we decided what to do.

Mick had lost his honour and his family in Ireland. I had lost my honour and my family in Scotland, as had Margaret. All three of us had lost our country too. So, countryless, honourless, but thankfully not penniless, we had some thinking to do about our next move. Then, one day in a London coffee-house, we met an Englishman called Peter Dicken, and once again, everything changed.

Chapter Eight – Mick To The Rescue

I'll never forget that fateful night that me and Jim went to the Tolbooth Inn to sort that Ogilvie fella out, but ended up staying for horizontal refreshments instead. Though sweet wee Jane was the first woman whose warmth that I had ever felt, the joy of that encounter isn't my strongest memory of that evening or the events that occurred directly afterwards. What I'll always remember most about all that is the feeling of strange dread that I had when Jim asked me to go and round up Smith, Grant and Munro from our building squad for our wee 'bit of business' that we had planned for the next day. I really didn't want to leave Jim in the Inn, it felt wrong and I feared that I would never see him again. He was my only true friend in Edinburgh though – we got on well, we had a lot in common and we had a lot of laughs. He and his family were good to me in so many ways, and I tried to be the best friend that I could to him, that's why I went against my gut-feeling and disappeared into the night that evening, leaving him with Ogilvie's daughter, Margaret. She too was a fine lookin' lass, but I wouldn't have trusted her as far as I could have thrown her. After I left the Inn, I went straight to the boarding house where Smith, Grant and Munro were lodged. They were good lads, like us, they were on Ogilvie's 'blacklist', so we always stood by each other. Unfortunately, on this occasion, I feel that I let them down, badly. I was delayed on my way to their lodgings when the contents of a chamber-pot emptied onto my head, followed by a half-hearted warning cry of 'Garde de l'eau' from the tenement above. I don't know what that person had been eating, but their excrement was particularly vile, making me retch as I frantically tried to wipe the disgusting shite from my hair and face with my pocket handkerchief. The piss and shite seemed to be in my nose, up it, everywhere basically. I shouted some abuse at whoever it was that had dumped their chamber pot on my head, and continued on my way, I had only been delayed by a few moments, but that delay was to prove important.

There was quite a commotion going on at the boarding house when I got there. What looked like a lynch-mob was assembled outside my workmates' lodgings, and carrying pistols, they were forcing Smith, Grant and Munro into a carriage. The lads were objecting loudly, but they were outnumbered 10-3 by whoever the lynch mob was. Straight away I knew that it was Ogilvie's boys. I'm ashamed to admit that I did nothing – I was still carrying the blade that Jim had given me but I knew that one blade against ten pistols would be a futile, if heroic, gesture. Instead, I crept closer and listened to what was being said.

Our three lads appeared to be being forcibly removed from Edinburgh. I didn't recognise the two older men who were doing most of the talking, but I listened.

They spoke loudly to Smith, Grant and Munro, by now all bundled into the carriage, which was now flanked by six pistol-carrying horsemen. The two older men who were doing most of the talking told our boys that ' they were lucky that they weren't to be killed', but that if they ever dared return to Edinburgh, that's exactly what would happen to them. They were also warned that if they somehow managed to avoid being put on the ship at Leith, their landlady – who was sobbing in the house's doorway- would be killed, and her daughter, whom Munro had taken a shine to, would end up working as a whore in Ogilvie's Inn. It was then that I realised what was really going on – Ogilvie was getting rid of mine and Jim's backup. I reckoned that they were being dumped on a boat at Leith which would take them far away from Edinburgh, and I was right. Flanked by the six armed horsemen and looking very sullen, even in the moonlight, the small procession made its way off into the dark, smelly, Edinburgh night towards Leith, and that's the last that I ever saw of my old workmates. I felt, impotent, useless, cowardly even – I hadn't been able to do anything. This left four men outside what had previously been my friends' lodgings. I couldn't really tell who the two older men who appeared to be in charge were, it was dark and both were in tall hats. I saw one of them approach the lady whose lodging house it was and give her what looked like a bag of money, saying in a sneering voice 'for your trouble'. The poor sobbing old woman took the money but shook her head disdainfully at the men, who simply laughed and turned to walk away – in the opposite direction from where I was. They spoke briefly to the two younger men on horses as they left, sending them off into the night. I burned with rage, but I saw my chance – the odds were now only 2-1 against me, and me being an Irishman, those were good odds!

With the two older men walking away from me, I crept out of the shadows and walked after them, my hand on my blade. I used all of my stealth to get as close to them as possible, but when I got to within ten paces of them, they somehow heard me and spun around – one with a leveled flintlock pistol and the other with a rather nasty long blade which he had produced from a sword-cane. To my dismay I realised that they weren't as old as I thought they were – in the murky light they appeared to be in their mid 30's, much younger than I had hoped. One had a moustache, the other a beard. The bearded one with the pistol spoke.

'Well, well well, if it isn't that bog-trotter from Reid's squad – typical taig eh? Brings a knife to a gun-fight'.

Both of them laughed, I was temporarily rooted to the spot. The bearded one continued.

'We weren't going to kill you, we know all about that murder you committed in Sligo last year, Warfield, we were going to leave you for her majesty's constables to arrest tomorrow, but, since you're here now'.

The bearded one fired his pistol at me and missed completely, even at a ten-pace range, I don't even think he had loaded it properly, but that didn't matter. As he fumbled to reload his pistol and his mustachioed friend stood hesitantly holding his sword cane, I had a decision to make. Should I stab the pistol carrier then take out the sword-cane man, or vice versa? In the end, they made my decision for me- but these slightly overweight Scotsmen made one crucial error – they forgot that I am Irish.

I've scarce had an easier fight in my life. As the bearded one tried to reload his pistol so that he could fire it again, I threw my knife at him, knocking the pistol out of his hand. I was right behind the thrown knife and had soon disarmed the one with the sword cane, then it was just a matter of giving them a few slaps.

By a few slaps, I mean I battered them senseless. They were begging me to stop, but I didn't feel in the mood for showing mercy after the spectacle that I had just been witness to. It took Mrs.

Jardine, the lodging house's landlady, to get me to stop before I killed them. It was evident that both of the men were drunk, so I simply dragged them into a nearby close and left them there, alive but near unconscious.

Mrs. Jardine invited me into her house and gave me some soup and bread, and then told me everything. I was only half-listening, as by then I had remembered what the two men had said about me and Sligo, they even knew my name, but Mrs. Jardine told me that Jim had indeed been 'set-up' by Ogilvie's mob and could expect a visit from them early the next morning. My first instinct was to rush back to The Tolbooth Inn to rescue Jim from this elaborate trap, but Mrs. Jardine convinced me to wait in her house until first light. I took the pistol that the bearded man had been carrying, along with four cartridges from his pocket, and then I gave both men a good whack on the head with the pistol-butt, leaving them unconscious in the neighbouring close. I stayed at Mrs. Jardine's until morning. She gave me the small purse of money that Ogilvie's henchmen had given her as 'compensation' for evicting her boarders.

At first I refused to take it, but Mrs. Jardine explained that she wanted to help us, but also that she would have to tell the city police that I had robbed her as well, to avoid repercussions from Ogilvie's men, so I agreed. Then, that morning, I arrived in the nick of time at The Tolbooth Inn to save my friend Jim from Ogilvie and his sons. I've no idea what happened to the two nasty fellas I left unconscious in that close, and I didn't really care what happened to them either – they were bullies, they deserved it. Ironically though, if one of them had been a bit more skillful with firearms, I might not have had a pistol with which to rescue Jim from The Tolbooth.

And so me, Jim and that Margaret one had to do a runner to London – my second 'runner' in a year.

I really hated her at first, but Jim seemed to have forgiven her and knew much more about her than I did, so I tried to give her the benefit of the doubt. They remained lovers. The hotel we lodged in in London was a bit dirty, but at least it was safe – for now. No questions asked. I can't say that I missed Edinburgh one bit – in essence it hadn't been much different from my own Sligo, greedy landlords and businessmen riding rough-shod over the ordinary hardworking people, while the law and authorities either looked the other way or actively encouraged them. That's not to say that I wasn't thankful for some parts of my brief life in Edinburgh. I had learned a lot about how my fellow countrymen were treated in the countries that they fled Ireland to, and if the filthy, disease ridden Cowgate was anything to go by, things weren't much better away from Ireland than in it. But I had also made a true Scottish friend in Jim Reid – both of us had lost brothers, but we were kind of like adopted brothers by now and as I say, we had a lot in common.

The train journey to London was very boring. Jim and Margaret did all of the talking, just in case anyone was looking for us and heard my Irish accent. We had plenty of money and Margaret soon got herself a respectable but low-paid job in the hotel we were staying in, a job that came with permanent lodgings.

Then we met Peter Dicken…

Chapter Nine – The Englishman

The Hotel Talavera, where Jim, Margaret and Mick were staying – named after an English victory over France some 50 years earlier- was little more than two converted London town houses knocked into one building. After Margaret began working there to pay her board, the place got cleaner and started to be run more efficiently. One night after dinner, when Margaret was away working in the kitchens, Mick and Jim were approached by an Englishman, bald, in his early thirties, who offered to buy them a drink at a nearby pub. Mick and Jim agreed and the three men made the short journey a few hundred yards down the road to The Crown pub, where they drank gin and introduced themselves.

The Englishman, who had arrived at the hotel only a few days after Mick and Jim, introduced himself as Peter Dicken, formerly of Yorkshire. He said that he had just arrived from Edinburgh, which made both Mick and Jim a tad suspicious at first, but they were oddly relieved and even slightly amused when he confessed that he had left Edinburgh to escape 'a young lady in Leith with a swollen belly and an angry father'. He then, for no apparent reason, brought out a small blue velvet purse, and after glancing over his shoulder, opened it and showed its contents to Mick and Jim. Both men's eyes were out on stalks – the purse contained four beautiful diamonds!

Dicken then dropped a bombshell.

'I'm guessing that you're the two men Edinburgh's city police are looking for in connection with the robbery and death of that 'orrible Mr. Ogilvie and his sons? A Jock and a Paddy. Well well boys, you did right getting out of there. You'd have long since swung had you stayed in Edinburgh lads. Pity about Ogilvie's daughter though, I was told she was a beauty'.

Stunned, Jim and Mick didn't know what to say next, but Dicken continued.

'Though I'm guessing that it wasn't really the body of Ogilvie's daughter they found in that burned out Inn – more likely it was one of the serving girls whom Ogilvie or his sons had killed in an attempt to set you chaps up, am I right? In which case, your Margaret is Ogilvie's 'dead' daughter. Am I correct?'

Jim and Mick looked at each other, and then simply nodded, before Jim spoke.

'Well Mr. Dicken, you're quite the detective. If you know all that then you'll also know that anything we did was in defence of ourselves and our friends and family, Ogilvie was a bastard, all his lot were.'

Dicken was quick to reply.

'Oh yes, most of Edinburgh's relieved that him and his sons are gone. Actually, that same night, a gang of Irishmen beat Ogilvie's two cousins near to death as well.'

Mick laughed. He still hadn't told Jim about that episode at the lodging house, but he spoke.

'A gang was it? No lad, it was just me who did that, on my own, after I had disarmed them'.

Mick paused as he felt Jim's steely gaze bore into him. Dicken was laughing, and clearly believed Mick's version of events. But Mick and Jim then tried to tread more carefully. Jim spoke.

'So, Mr. Dicken'.

'Please chaps, call me Peter' said Dicken.

'Alright then, Peter. How do you know all of this? And what's it all got to do with those Diamonds that you have? Are you here to turn us in? Why were you in Edinburgh?'

'And no bloody riddles' added Mick.

Dicken laughed, then shouted to the serving girl for more gin, which was soon brought over and drunk by all three men, then Dicken spoke.

'I suppose I do owe you boys an explanation, and a straight-talking one. I know all of this because I was supposed to deliver these here diamonds to Mr. Ogilvie the day after that fire – he had a passion for precious stones you see, I think these are worth at least £4000. But of course, neither Ogilvie nor any of his associates was available to make the exchange, so I suppose these are mine now. I assure you that I'm not here to turn you in. I suppose that I must come-clean, gentlemen. I am currently on promenade!'

'Do you mean on holiday?' asked Jim.

'No, no no. I'm a deserter from The French Foreign Legion, a soldier of fortune. I deserted in 1858 after the last of my comrades was killed in a Tuareg ambush in Algeria. I was literally the last man left in my company. I played dead and was thought so by the Tuareg. An Arab scout rescued me in the desert and together we managed to escape first to Spain, then France. The Arab scout is waiting for me in Paris with the last of the diamonds, one more; he has it as our 'insurance'. I call him Roumis, but that's not his real name – it's a kind of joke- Roumis is the derogatory name that the Arabs call Legionnaires. I can't actually pronounce his real name, and in any case, he seems to like Roumis.'

'Why did you join France's army?' asked Jim.

'Well, it's simple – I had to get out of the country when I was aged 18, after a minor misdemeanor' said Dicken.

'Misdemeanor?' asked Mick.

Dicken sighed, and then spoke.

'I had a disagreement with the greedy bastard who owned the Mill where everyone in my hometown in Yorkshire worked, after he tried to cut wages. A disagreement that he lost, on account of my punching his lights out!'

Jim and Mick both laughed and smiled. Dicken continued.

'I hit the bastard too hard, ten minutes after I hit him he collapsed, stone dead, with blood pouring from his ears and mouth – it was an accident – but who was going to take my word over that of his family and his lackeys? No-one, that's who. I'd have been hanged'.

Mick and Jim finally saw why Dicken had approached them; he was in exactly the same boat as them. Jim was the next to speak.

'So Peter, I'm guessing that you have a plan?'

'Yes I do as it happens. I need to get to Paris, soon, and then I need to dispose of these diamonds.

But it's a valuable load that I carry – I need security, if you know what I mean, and from what I've heard, you two are just the kind of men that I need. What say you? There's a fair cut of the diamond profits in it for you.'

Mick then spoke.

'Looks like we don't have any choice now, between the three of us we're wanted in all three kingdoms of the British Isles for murder or robbery. What do you think Jim? Paris? No more stinking Thames wafting up our nostrils each day.'

'Aye' said Jim, seeing that it was their only option. 'But first we have to tell Margaret that she's not 'dead' in Edinburgh, if you know what I mean'.

'Agreed' said Mick. 'When do we leave, Peter?'

Dicken answered 'first thing tomorrow. Much appreciated gentlemen, thank you. You won't regret this.'

'You will, if you mess us around' said Jim.

There was a brief silence before the three men laughed, drank some more gin, then headed back to their hotel – tomorrow would bring a new adventure.

Chapter Ten - Decisions

Though the timing of his finding us was rather odd, we were nevertheless happy to escort Dicken to Paris. Mick thought he seemed like 'one of us', whatever that meant, while I saw Dicken as an escape route for us all. We couldn't just remain in London, the money we stole in Edinburgh wouldn't last us forever. I was a little saddened when Margaret told us that she wasn't coming with us, but I already suspected that she wouldn't once we told her about how wee Jane's body had been mistaken for hers after the Tolbooth fire. Then to our utter disgust the next morning, we realised that Margaret was gone! She had ran away during the night, but not before relieving me of all of the sovereigns that we had ,while I was sleeping off the previous evening's gin! If it wasn't for Mick's money we would have been well and truly stuffed. Mick and I didn't think she'd go back to Edinburgh and betray us, but we couldn't risk hanging around London now, just in case.

And so it was that the Scotsman, the Irishman and the Englishman left London together, and four days later we were in Paris, the most beautiful city in the world.

Our stay in Paris began reasonably well. We spent the first week doing nothing but eating, drinking and whoring, and we had a mighty fine time. Paris made Edinburgh look like an open sewer. The prostitutes and cafes soon ate into what money we had left, and we began to ask Dicken exactly when he was planning to sell the diamonds and give us our cut, and we asked who he had obtained them from in the first place. Our first question was soon answered when Dicken finally met up with his Arab chum, Roumis. Mick and I liked Roumis from the start. He had a smattering of English, as well as a decent grasp of French, which helped, as Dicken spoke French fairly well. Roumis never drank alcohol as he was a Muslim, his thing was coffee and whoring. As for Dicken, we took to our English friend well, he was a clever man, very funny, but we also got the impression that he'd be good to have around if we ever got into a spot of trouble, and above all, we trusted him. In fact, it was clear to us early on that Mr. Dicken was a well-educated man, whatever his background, and we knew that would come in useful.

One evening we asked Roumis why he had left Algeria. He wouldn't answer us directly, but he did say that he had did something foolish over a woman, and had been made outcast by even his own family and had 'dishonoured' himself. Dicken later told us that he had bedded the wife of his brother.

One Saturday morning, when we had almost run out of money, Dicken dragged us down to a dodgy looking pawnbroker's in Montmartre, to finally sell the diamonds. Just before we entered the shop, Dicken told us that the diamonds in fact belonged to a Paris merchant by the name of Markov, and that he had simply been the courier – however, as he had received no payment in Edinburgh, on account of Ogilvie being dead, he had decided to keep the diamonds in lieu of pay. This made Mick and I very uneasy, but as we were about to sell the stones, we put it to the back of our minds. As we entered the pawnbroker's, the small bespectacled shopkeeper waved his arm and shouted ' non, non, non Arbis' , meaning that he didn't want Roumis in his shop, so Roumis, a tall- slim young Arab man with a scarred neck, waited outside as we conducted our business.

The little pawnbroker took his time examining the stones with his special eye-glass. We could tell he thought they were the real deal, but the deal he offered Dicken was far from satisfactory – less than half of what he had hoped for, which would mean that we all got less money for our trouble. It was as if the pawnbroker knew that we were desperate. Reluctantly, Dicken agreed to his lower price, but there was a sting in the tail – we would have to wait half an hour for our money, as the pawnbroker said that he didn't keep such vast amounts on his premises. We were fine with that, it was only 30 minutes after all. More fool us.

After about 40 minutes, the pawnbroker's young assistant came running into the shop and handed three big sacks of Francs to his boss, who in turn handed the sacks to Dicken, who counted the money, and then nodded to us to follow him out of the shop. We thanked the pawnbroker, who barely looked up from his ledgers. When we got outside, we saw Roumis to the door's left, with his back to the wall, a big Frenchman holding a blade to his throat, but we could not intervene. We were confronted with seven armed men and one older man carrying a cane. The seven men all had revolvers drawn, and to my astonishment, three of them were policemen, wearing the uniform of the French Police Nationale.

The man with the cane introduced himself as 'Monsieur Markov' and demanded that we hand over the Francs, and any other valuables that we had – We had been set up by the pawnbroker!

Mick, Dicken and I glanced at each other, ready to fight against the men even though they were armed and we were not, but then we heard Roumis yelp as one of Markov's thugs cut off part of his ear. Realising the futility of resisting, with a sigh, Dicken threw the bags of Francs onto the ground, and then we emptied our pockets of any extra money that we had. We felt so helpless, so impotent, so dishonoured, but once we had given them everything that we had, they let Roumis go, and then they simply departed. It seemed that we were double-damned – we'd lost the diamonds AND the money.

Surprisingly, given the collective trail of destruction that Dicken, Mick and I had left in our wake in Britain, we took this blow extremely well at first, but then, it dawned on us. In Paris with no money:

Where would we sleep?

How would we eat?

How could we find work when only two of us spoke French?

Paris was already full of jobless foreign beggars, none of us wanted to be like them. As we sullenly walked away, Dicken spoke.

'We must have work, we must have money, and bread, and a way out of Paris.'

Mick and I asked him just how we were supposed to get all of these things.

Dicken replied. 'It's simple, my friends. There's no other option. We join the Foreign Legion'.

Roumis was the only one of us who hadn't had his pockets rifled by Markov's thugs, so with his last few Sous we got ourselves some soup and coffee at a café about a mile from Montmartre. We talked.

I asked Dicken how on earth he would be able to join The Legion if he was already a deserter from it. Dicken replied that the legion thought that he was dead with all his other comrades in that ambush, so he couldn't see that being a problem, particularly as he had enlisted under a false name the first time. Dicken also told us that he was finished – the diamonds had been his last chance of making a go of civilian life. We talked for a good while.

'All this way to end up broke and joining the French Army' said Mick, in a downbeat tone. Dicken corrected him.

'It's not the French Army – you have to be French to join the Imperial Army. It's The Legion – foreigners only – you fight for the Legion's honour, and for your comrades, but, you are still fighting France's battles.'

Mick answered.

'After the last two years grief, joining the French Foreign Legion doesn't sound so bad, I'm in! I wouldn't be the first Irishman to fight for France, would I?'

'Nor I the first Scot' I added.

'And I already know the ropes, if we stick together it'll be fine chaps – a hard life, but far away from our troubles' said Dicken before turning to Roumis.

Roumis simply nodded and managed to say 'Yes, Oui', whilst he passed something to Dicken, which Dicken put into his pocket. We thought nothing of it at the time.

'What if they won't take Roumis on account of his race?' I asked Dicken.

'It'll be alright' he replied.' We'll just tell the recruiting office that if they don't take him, they lose us all'.

And so the four of us trudged off towards the Legion's Paris recruiting depot. For different reasons, we had all failed in life. We had lost our families, become estranged from our homes, in our cultures we had committed what some would consider to be heinous crimes, we were penniless and would soon be starving, and above all, the four of us had lost our sense of self worth and worst of all, lost our honour. And so our minds were made up – we were going to join the Foreign Legion

Chapter Eleven- Taking The Sous

And so it was that the Scotsman, the Irishman, the Englishman and their Arab friend walked off Paris's streets and through the door of one of Paris's two recruiting offices for the Foreign Legion, or Légion Etrangère, on the Rue Sainte Dominique.

A small bell above the door rang as Dicken opened the door and entered, followed by Mick, Jim and Roumis. To their right was a tiny office that was more like a kiosk. At the kiosk's window sat a small, red-faced man in military uniform who was busily sifting through the pile of paperwork in front of him, not even lifting his gaze when he heard the bell on the door ring and the four men entering the office.

The rest of the room was bare and simple. There were two doors out of the main room, one of which was marked 'medecin', meaning doctor, the other marked simply with 'Officier - 'Défense d'entrer' – Officer – Keep out'.

There were eight empty chairs in the main office foyer, just to the left of the kiosk at the door.

Only Dicken and Roumis spoke French, Dicken slightly better-so than Roumis, as Roumis had only ever needed to know 'Legion French' – enough French to understand the basic commands of an officer or NCO. This being the case, the four men had previously agreed that Dicken should do all the talking at first. As the four men waited patiently at the kiosk, the soldier, a Sergeant-Major, completely ignored them, carrying on with his paperwork, stamping sheets of paper, making notes and generally looking in every direction except at the four men. After a few minutes of waiting, Dicken coughed loudly, as if he was clearing his throat. Still, the Sergeant-Major did not look up from his paperwork, making it obvious that he was ignoring them. Dicken coughed again, loudly, and more obviously, in order to gain the little man's attention. Without looking up, the Sergeant Major, or 'Chef', finally answered.

'You should perhaps see a doctor my friend – monsieur would appear to have something wrong with his throat'.

Dicken's response was witty and swift.

'And monsieur would appear to have something wrong with his ears, no?'

The Chef banged on his desk and finally looked up to see the four men standing at his kiosk, then spoke.

'Ah, we seem to have four comedians here, are you sure you have come to the right place?' he asked sarcastically.

Dicken ignored the sarcastic comment and spoke plainly but politely to the little Sergeant-Major.

'We wish to join the Legion'.

The Sergeant-Major smiled, looked at the four of them, and then spoke in a tone that addressed all four men.

'Well, I didn't think you had come here to play Tennis, mes amis. Doubtless you will have many such laughs at the expense of your copains and your officers, being such comedians, no?'

The four men stood silent for a moment, all four of them fearing that they had already blown their chances of joining up. Then the Chef spoke again.

'We are not accepting new recruits at this office at the moment, my friends, I fear that you may have had a wasted journey- but I will just go and double-check with Major Blanc - we did lose rather a lot of men at Magenta and in Africa recently- you will all wait over there – move'.

The Chef pointed towards the wooden chairs in the middle of the room before he disappeared into the officer's office for a moment, before re-emerging, to address the four of them, in a slightly cheerier tone. He pointed to Jim first – 'You, go in there' he said, pointing to the door that led into the officer's office.

Jim nodded and got up, Mick winked at him, and then Jim disappeared through the door, closing it behind him.

At the table in the office sat Major Blanc, who looked in his early 50's but still made an imposing figure with his medal-decorated chest and gold epaulettes. With a warm smile he invited Jim to take a seat opposite him at his desk.

'So my friend, you wish to join The Legion?'

'If The Legion will have me' answered Jim, keenly and politely. Major Blanc continued.

'Very well. We aren't supposed to be taking any new recruits at the moment, but you may be in luck – enlistments have been down since the Battle of Magenta, even though it was a great victory for our glorious French Empire!'

'What are the terms of enlistment?' asked Jim.

'You are keen aren't you? I suppose that's no bad thing. Very well. Your initial enlistment is for a period of five years, for service in Algeria or anywhere else that the Emperor decides to send you. For the right man there are opportunities for advancement, adventure, learning, comradeship and even decoration and promotion – you might be sergeant one day – maybe even Sergeant-Major, who knows. I warn you though my friend, it is a hard-life as well, one of monotonous duty punctuated only by moments of extreme terror. After five years' service, for which you will be paid one Sous a day, minus stoppages, you will be given the opportunity to enlist for another five years, and if you complete 15 years service you will be eligible for a more generous pension – though few men survive to collect the basic pension – let alone that one. Does that sound like the kind of life that you want, monsieur…what is your name?'

Jim had to think fast, and he stuttered, and then said the first name that popped into his head.

'Jimmy, Sir, Mr. Jimmy'

Major Blanc laughed, and then spoke, still retaining his friendly, fatherly tone.

'A Scotsman called Mr. Jimmy? Well I have heard sillier names, most of them fake, to be fair – I assume that you too are enlisting under a nom de guerre – an assumed name? I will of course ask no awkward questions, C'est La Legion!'

Major Blanc wrote 'Jimmy' as the surname on Jim's enlistment form, then pushed the form across the desk so that Jim could fill out the rest of it. Jim picked up the pen and filled in the two-sided form as quickly as he could, but when he got to the very end of the form and was about to sign his new 'name', Major Blanc reached across and stopped his hand, speaking in a slightly sterner voice.

'Bear in mind that once you have signed this form, assuming that the doctor declares you fit to serve, you will be a duly enlisted soldier of the French Empire, under martial-law and without any right of appeal whatsoever. You cannot buy yourself out or be bought out by anyone else, nor can your country's Consul help you in any way until you have fulfilled your contract of five years. However, after five years you can become a naturalised French citizen, and can choose to keep your new name, or revert to your old identity. Oh, and don't even think about going on promenade , deserters from The Legion are shot without trial, unless the desert or the Arabs get them first. There are only three ways that you can leave The Legion legally- fulfill your contract, get wounded so badly that you become a cripple, or die in the service of France and The Legion - Do you still wish to enlist, Mr. Jimmy?'

Jim answered 'Yes, Sir', which put a smile on the Major's face before he continued speaking.

'Very well, before you sign your name, please take a short walk through the doctor's door at the other side of the main office out there, take off your clothes and put on one of the dressing gowns and wait for the doctor to examine you – but I think you have nothing to worry about on that front. Those other three men outside, they are friends of yours?'

'Yes, Sir' answered Jim.

'I will try to see that you serve together' said Major Blanc. 'Send the red-haired one in next'.

Jim stood up and turned around, then walked out of that office, gesturing to Mick to go in next.

Then Jim went through to the doctor's office, and stripped, as required. His examination was conducted by a small, bald doctor who reeked of Cognac, and it wasn't much of an examination. He had to read an eye chart, cough while his chest was being sounded, and he had his teeth examined. The doctor, who barely said a word to him, gave him a certificate, then told him to change back into his own clothes and go back to wait in the main office beside the others. Just as Jim was leaving the doctor's office, Mick entered, looking excited, and they exchanged winks. When Jim sat down again in the main office, only Roumis was there – Dicken was in with Major Blanc.

After a nervous wait of a few minutes, Dicken emerged from Blanc's office and strode across to the doctor's office, looking more relieved than pleased, just as Mick emerged from the doctor's, also carrying a certificate like the one Jim had. Dicken was in and out of the doctor's office even more quickly than Jim or Mick, also with a certificate. Roumis hadn't been called into Blanc's office though, so Dicken asked the Chef at the kiosk why Roumis was still waiting. The Sergeant-Major replied that the Major would be out to see them presently. The four men waited in silence, for five minutes that seemed like an eternity. Finally, Major Blanc emerged from his office, carrying four enlistment forms, and sat down with the men, placing the un-signed forms and a pen on the small table beside the chairs. He then spoke.

'Congratulations my friends, it seems that you have all passed your medicals, all I need is your signatures on these forms and you will immediately be soldiers of France.'

'What about him?' said Dicken, pointing at Roumis, who was fidgeting uneasily.

'I'm afraid we can't take your Arab friend as a Legionnaire. It would upset morale when you get to Algeria.'

Dicken then did something remarkable, which the others thought would jeopardise all of their chances of joining. He picked up the four enlistment forms in one hand, and spoke firmly and directly to Major Blanc.

'Well, Major, you know my story, and his, from our little chat earlier. If you don't take Roumis, you lose all four of us, we walk out of here as civilians.'

'You mean as beggars!' scoffed Blanc. Dicken spoke again.

'We'd rather be beggars than leave our friend behind. It's the four of us, or none of us, Sir'.

Major Blanc looked stony faced for a while, then laughed and replied.

'Now that's the spirit of The Legion, my friends. No true Legionnaire ever deserts his copain (comrade). Very well, you shall all be enlisted today. Sign and date these forms please, gentlemen. Chef!'

The Sergeant-Major from the kiosk was at the Major's side within seconds of being summoned, moving remarkably quickly for such a small, older man. Jim, Mick, Dicken, and Roumis all signed the forms and passed them back to Blanc, who laughed when he saw the name 'Roumis' on their Arab friend's form. Major Blanc shook all four of their hands, and then disappeared back into his office after wishing the four men 'bonne chance' (good luck).

The four men then heard the Chef roar 'garde-à-vous' (attention), and all four men did their best to stand to attention and listened to the little Sergeant-Major.

'You are now soldiers of France. You will catch the evening train to Marseille, where you will report immediately to Fort St Jean, where you will then be embarked for Oran. It is not hard to find the fort.

I will give you your travel orders and meal allowance for the journey, and your new identity papers, you had best hurry, the next train leaves in just over one hour.'

'Thank you, Chef' said Dicken, saluting him. Jim, Mick and Roumis then saluted him too, looking a tad silly doing so in shabby civilian clothes. The Sergeant-Major then offered the four men some advice before they left.

'Now listen, the best advice that I can give you is this. The Legion may be commanded by officers, but it is run by Sergeants and Corporals. Disobey your conscience or your God if you will, but NEVER disobey your NCO's. To you, they are God. Listen, learn, keep yourself, your musket and your caserne (barracks) very clean, watch each other's backs, and beware of local drink and local women. One final warning – don't steal. If there's one thing Legionnaires hate, it's thieves. If you steal, you'll most likely end up pinned to the barrack table one night with bayonets through your hands and ears. Now go, The Legion is your country now – I pray that you serve your country well. Au revoir!'

And with that, the four men saluted the little Sergeant-Major, turned, and left the recruiting office, heading for the railway station. As they left, the Chef shouted after them. 'And remember, no-one likes a comedian!'

Chapter Twelve– Into The Unknown

Our journey from Paris to Marseille was as uneventful as our journey to London from Scotland had been, though this time we had a lot to talk about. We travelled third-class, and our meal allowance wasn't very generous, but we at least had something to occupy our minds – chiefly picking Dicken's brains about life in The Legion. It turned out he was indeed quite the Oracle, and Mick, Roumis and I felt better knowing that we had him to show us the ropes. We were off on a great adventure, to North Africa to fight the Arabs. It was getting dark when we reached Marseille and got our first glimpse of the silhouette of Fort St Jean, which we reached with little trouble, other than being footsore and hungry, but we all supposed that that was to be our lot from now on. A rather grumpy Corporal directed us to our dormitory, where we were to spend one night before taking ship to Oran the very next day. Mick and I were disappointed in that we weren't given uniforms or weapons in Marseille, though we were grateful for the soup, bread and coffee that we were given the morning after we arrived, just before we, and about 200 other new recruits, were marched down to the harbour, still in our shabby civilian clothes, to take ship for Oran.

Mick was taken badly with sea-sickness during the fairly short crossing of the Mediterranean, but like with everything else in life, he put up with it. On the ship we talked. As it turned out, Mick had been just as nervous as me when he had enlisted, and had given his surname as 'Mick', so now we really were 'Mick and Jimmy'. Roumis had of course used his adopted name, 'Roumis', and Dicken had enlisted using his real name, having used an assumed name during his first spell in The Legion. When I asked Dicken how he had managed to disguise the fact that he was already a deserter from The Legion, he admitted that he hadn't been able to. Major Blanc had known that he had served before, just by looking at him, but Major Blanc hadn't bothered one bit. Dicken said Blanc had admitted that he was happy to regain a trained soldier, and had also been pragmatic, pointing out that there really was nothing that he could do to Dicken even if he had deserted before. In that sense, we had been lucky. We spent an uncomfortable night at the baking-hot Fort St Theresa at Oran after disembarking, before we were all crammed into smelly, dirty cattle trains and slowly taken the 40 or so miles to The Legion's headquarters- the great fortress and town of Sidi-Bel-Abbes – where we would begin our training and finally be able to trade in our own shabby clothes for the blue and white uniform, Kepi (cap with cloth or couvre to protect the neck and ears from the sun) and blue abdominal sash of The Legion. Here, we would also learn how to be soldiers...

Chapter Thirteen– A Harsh Reality

It wasn't until basic training began that Mick and Jimmy realised fully what they had signed five years of their lives away for. From day one in Sidi-Bel-Abbes the new recruits were subjected to the full rigours, privations and hardships combined with training and indoctrination that all recruits had to endure.

At first, they were delighted. They were issued with new, tough hobnail boots, woolen socks, two white linen suits, red pantaloons, a blue abdominal sash and the much anticipated heavy blue overcoat.

At first neither of them could understand the reasoning behind issuing soldiers who fought in the searingly hot African desert with a big, heavy overcoat, especially a dark blue one, but the reason for the overcoat became clear to both men fairly quickly. It wasn't just because France's army traditionally wore blue. Dicken, who had of course been in The Legion before, told them how perverse the climate in the desert could be – often baking hot in daytime but then utterly freezing at night, and as they trained, Mick and Jimmy began to understand- a heavy overcoat was actually of immense use in the desert, not just at night to keep out the freezing cold, but also for when resting during the day, as the coat absorbed a lot of the sun's heat which would otherwise have seriously damaged their skin through their white linen suits. The overcoats also had another advantage – though practically useless camouflage-wise at short to medium distance, at least the dark colour didn't reflect the sun's rays so that they could be seen at greater distances by the enemy.

All of the new recruits were buoyed on the second day of basic training, when they were each issued with what was to be their weapon- the 1859 MLE rifled-musket. It wasn't too heavy to carry at just five kilos, and came with a beautiful sword-bayonet, which attached to the fitting on the muzzle of the rifle with a simple twist, to be used as and when required. The rifle itself was a fine piece of military science, a vast improvement on the older, smoothbore percussion muskets. The rifled-musket fired the Minie bullet, a soft lead slug almost an inch in length – a fearsome projectile. The Minie bullet had been developed by a French officer of that name some years before, and was a vast improvement on the old spherical musket-balls. The combination of this new bullet and of the addition of rifling to rifle barrels, had revolutionised the role of the infantryman, and forever changed the role of the cavalryman.

The rifled-musket had been adopted because France's soldiers had frequently found that their old smoothbore muskets were easily outranged by the longer, more accurate home-made firearms carried by the Berber, The Tuareg and by their other colonial enemies. This had led to some serious reverses in The Legion's early days in North Africa, when defensive squares of Legionnaires had simply had their strength whittled down by enemy long range fire, before the depleted squares were simply ridden down by The Arabs. The rifled-musket's full potential was not fully realised until French and British troops, both armed with the weapon, had decimated their Russian enemies at long-range in the early stages of The Crimean War of 1854-56, when the Tsar's armies were still armed with Napoleonic –era smoothbore muskets. The rifled musket really was a revolution – whereas the old smoothbores had only been accurate at twenty or thirty paces and effective up to about 100-150 yards when fired in volleys, the newer rifled-musket was accurate at 250 yards, and even effective at a range of up to half a mile.

The MLE and its variants changed everything. On the continent, cavalry charges against infantry were now almost completely redundant – they had been effective against men whose only defence was a volley at 100 yards and then having to resort to the bayonet, but now the advantage was with the infantryman. All major European armies had by now discarded the old square formation for receiving cavalry charges, though these same armies were forced to retain the square as an option when fighting indigenous colonial enemies, who more often than not, surrounded and greatly outnumbered them.

The rifle was loaded by taking a pre-made linen or paper cartridge containing a bullet and a measure of black powder, biting off the bullet, pouring the black powder and the remains of the cartridge all the way down the muzzle of the rifle, then loading the bullet down the muzzle, ramming it home with a ramrod until the bullet sat on top of the powder in the barrel, and then finally, placing a percussion cap on the nipple at the weapon's lock, before cocking the hammer, and then it was ready to fire.

The Minie bullet itself was an horrific projectile. It caused horrendous, usually fatal wounds.

Although the Minie rifled-musket had much the same rate of fire as the old muskets-three to four shots per minute in the arms of a reasonably good man- being hit by a Minie bullet usually had one of four consequences.

If the victim was lucky, the bullet would simply slice his flesh, causing a painful, but treatable wound.

If the victim was unlucky enough to be shot in the arm or leg, the soft-lead slug would smash his bone, leading to almost certain amputation of the affected limb.

If the victim was unlucky enough to be shot in the chest or in the abdomen, the result was usually fatal, though death could sometimes take days.

If the victim was hit directly in the head, he was dead.

Not only was the bullet effective and accurate on impact, it also caused horrific exit wounds. Men shot in the torso would often have a small wound in their front and a much larger, gaping wound on their back, where the bullet had exited after tumbling inside their body.

In their first few days at Sidi-Bel-Abbes, Mick, Jimmy, Dicken, Roumis and the other new recruits were given a lecture about the brilliance of their new super-weapon by the officer in charge of their training, Captain Challier. Challier also drummed into the men that the rifle was merely their weapon, a tool of their trade, but that they should look after and take care of the beautiful rifle as if it was a family member. They were told to regularly clean and oil the weapon, they were taught to urinate down its barrel in emergencies if it ever became clogged with powder from too much firing in combat. And then, after these few days' lectures from Challier, they underwent a full week of field weapon stripping training, so that they knew their weapon inside out, and knew how to best maintain it. A vile sergeant named Lejaune and a corporal called Dupre – both Belgians – then became their drillmasters.

At first, training was monotonous but seemed fair. Not many of the recruits spoke French, so those who did were put into platoons with those who did not. Slowly, as the weeks passed, those who spoke no French began to learn the basics – Legion French – a few hundred essential words in French, words that wouldn't be useful anywhere in France other than in the army, or in a brothel.

As the language barrier was slowly broken down, so was the new recruits' sense of personal identity – this was nothing new and had been a tried and tested method of training soldiers since the days of Marius's Roman Army – and it was proven to work. What wasn't quite so tried and tested was the almost contemptuous attitude of the NCO's to the new recruits at Sidi. This varied in the Legion depending on just who those NCO's were, but in Mick and Jimmy's platoon, Sergeant Lejaune and Corporal Dupre walked a thin line between maintaining discipline and terrorising the men.

The men were roused by their NCO's at dawn, with a vicious tirade of verbal abuse, threats and shouting, the NCO's even kicking over anything in the caserne that would make a noise as they woke the men up. Before the men went on morning parade, they had to dress themselves, drink some thick, horrid coffee, clean and tidy their caserne (barracks) until it was spotless, and then make their way out for roll call. The NCOs picked up on anything as they inspected the men – dust on a button, a wrong fold in their linen suit, belt too tight, belt not tight enough, even if their as yet empty cartridge and cap pouches were slightly out of place, and above all, personal hygiene.

'A man who does not wash properly is a shame to himself and a danger of disease to his comrades, remember, you miserable sweepings of the gutters of Europe, you are Legionnaires now. Forget who you were, or think you were. Your faith may be in God but your pathetic backsides belong to me and Corporal Dupre' screamed Lejaune almost every morning on the parade ground.

After roll call, the men got their breakfast. 'Breakfast' was a dark euphemism for the whole platoon double-marching or running around the barracks, the base and even the walls in full kit, in the searing heat, to the screams of 'vite, vite' from their NCOs. Though exhausting and draining, this 'breakfast' was vital to the men's aclimatisation.

It all wore the men down. Often the NCO's would inspect the caserne after it had been cleaned and then, no matter what its state of actual cleanliness, would go berserk and insist that the men go back and clean it again. Anyone who objected or tried to protest was usually beaten by the NCOS, and after about a week, no-one ever complained to the NCOs again. Lejaune and Dupre also cleverly used peer-pressure to help lick the men into shape. If a man made an infraction, no matter how slight, his whole platoon was usually punished. This served both to double the men's resolve not to make infractions in the first place, but also instilled a bit of common pride and purpose in what the recruits did – and no man wanted to be the one responsible for his comrades being punished. Then there was the actual training.

The recruits never even fired their rifles in those first few weeks. They cleaned and oiled them, took them apart and put them back together, over and over again, day after day, only then to be told to shoulder their weapons for what was the Legion's main training method – marching.

At first the recruits marched a few miles in the morning, carrying full pack and rifle. Their whole load weighed up to 80lbs, and included not just their rifle, bayonet and ammunition, but also their mess tin, canteen of water, rations, trenching tool, blanket, tent and even a spare uniform. The men were only allowed to drink when Lejaune or Dupre said that they could – and even then, only one small cup at a time. If a man was caught drinking from his canteen when he wasn't supposed to be, he was severely punished, usually by being made to pour out the contents of his water bottle, hold his rifle above his head, and then run in a constant circuit on his own, wherever Lejaune or Dupre decided that he should do so, until he collapsed from heat and thirst, which in itself would incur a further punishment once the recruit had recovered.

This training, though cruel, had method to its madness. After training and being assigned to a company, Legionnaires would often have to march scores, even hundreds of miles to reach whatever God-forsaken outpost that they had been assigned to, and that took discipline, especially with regards to water. The distance that the recruits marched in basic training was steadily increased day-by-day, week by week, until the men could eventually march twenty miles a day with just a quart bottle of water to keep them from collapsing from thirst. They learned to drink wisely, and sparingly. Their lives depended on it. Running out of water in the desert meant death, either from thirst itself, or from the Arabs, who often picked off stragglers from Legion columns. Unless a man had been wounded in combat, if he collapsed and fell out of the column, he was disarmed of his rifle and bayonet and simply left to die, in most cases. The Legion wanted no new rifled-muskets falling into the Arabs' hands, and disarming a man who had collapsed was also a sure-fire way to tell if he was faking, intending to escape with his rifle to go on promenade, or in other words, to desert.

Roumis, Mick, Jimmy and Dicken had a common realisation of what they had done. They initially complained to each other often about their regret of signing up for five or more years of this.

Dupre seemed to have taken a dislike to Roumis purely on account of his Arab background, as had a number of the other recruits for the same reason. Mick, Dicken and Jimmy could easily protect their friend from the bullies in the ranks during what few hours that the men got to themselves back at Sidi after yet another long day's marching, but there was nothing that they could do when Dupre had a pop at him, often inventing excuses to punish the young Arab lad, and even beating him now and then.

They could do nothing about that. As far as they were concerned, Dupre and Lejaune were both their master and their God, with virtual power of life and death over them. Roumis himself did his best just to shrug it off and get on with training, but one evening after a particularly nasty punishment from Dupre, Roumis spoke to his three friends of desertion as they sat on their cots in the barracks. Jimmy and Mick didn't know what to say, but Dicken had some advice for Roumis, and for all three of them.

'Listen now lads, keep clean, do as you're told, and don't give those NCOs any excuse to get on your back. We're in Hell right now, but remember, I've did this before, it gets better.'

'When?' asked Roumis.

'Soon. Once we do the musketry course and the bayonet drill, that's pretty much it. You'll see. Besides, being here at Sidi isn't so bad – at least we won't get le Cafard here.'

'What is le Cafard?' asked Mick.

Chapter Fourteen– Le Cafard

Dicken smiled then answered. 'Le Cafard is a form of desert madness. It's most common on long marches or among those of us who are stationed in remote outposts where life is even more monotonous than it is here'.

He stopped smiling and spoke in a quieter, more serious tone.

'Le Cafard is like a beetle crawling around your brain. It crawls slowly at first. But, the greater the heat, the boredom, the monotony, the drink, the hopelessness, the faster it crawls. It makes good men attack their officer, or their copain, it makes them desert stark naked never to be seen again, and when the beetle's crawling gets ever faster, it can compel a man to stop the crawling by shooting himself in the brain, or opening his own guts up with his bayonet.'

'How do we avoid le Cafard?' asked Jimmy.

'You can't. For Europeans in the desert, le Cafard is everywhere. Roumis knows it, but will probably never be taken by it, but for the rest of us, it's a constant threat. Keep your mind occupied and pray not to be sent to some remote outpost in the south, and you may avoid le Cafard. The Arabs say that it is Allah's way of punishing us for occupying Arab lands.'

'Can it be cured?' asked Jimmy.

'If caught early and the man is taken out of the sun for a few weeks, it can be beaten. If not caught early, it will turn your brain to crawling maggots, my friend.'

Dicken had never been wrong about anything to do with the Legion that he had told his three friends, and they trusted his word. One thing was clear – no-one wanted to get le Cafard.

The daily marching and cleaning continued.

Day after sun-seared day.

When the recruits weren't out marching and running around in the hot, damned, dirty sand, or worse, running around with sacks of rocks on their backs, they were confined to the oven-like caserne at Sidi. The only time that they were given any real time to themselves, other than when they were asleep, was when they were paid and set loose on the populace of the town of Sidi-bel-Abbes. The town would fill with 'off-duty' Legionnaires and officers whenever the pay chests arrived and the men received the few sous that they had been tramping their feet off for. The Legionnaires usually wrecked the town on pay-day, the busy Arab market town soon becoming a huge open air orgy of drinking, gambling, whoring and fist fights. Often there was nothing that the High Command in Sidi could do except wait for the worst of the carnage to die down after a couple of days, and then send Gendarmes or other Legionnaires to arrest whatever rogue Legionnaires were still in the town, which was usually pretty badly smashed up by then. Legionnaires were even forbidden from taking their bayonets into town when off-duty, in case they got drunk and used them on either their comrades, or on the local populace. The next few days after pay-day would usually be busy ones for the Legion's doctors, as officers and men alike lined up to be treated for the variety of exotic and disgusting venereal diseases that they had contracted from the many whores in Sidi-Bel-Abbes, and to be patched up after drunken brawls with their copain or with angry locals.

After pay day, the men settled back into their monotonous routine. Their only meal was soup, bread and coffee, served two times daily. The coffee was thick and disgusting, but there was plenty of it. The bread was grey, tough and tasteless, but again, there was always plenty of it. 'Soup' or 'Soupe' was a mixture of meat, macaroni, pieces of biscuit and whatever vegetables the Legion's cooks were able to lay their hands on, the latter in order to prevent scurvy. This diet was high in carbohydrate, which gave the Legionnaires plenty of energy, but also left them feeling hungry for much of the time. The Legionnaires also had a daily ration of pinard, a kind of sickly-sweet but strong red wine, though to call such a substance 'wine' was to insult every vineyard in Burgundy and Bordeaux. Nevertheless, they drank it, it wasn't too strong, but it did the job.

One morning, Lejaune and Dupre woke the barracks up at dawn by screaming 'Aux Armes, Aux Armes, Les Arbis!', indicating that Sidi was under attack by Arabs. The panic-stricken, half-awake recruits were dressed and on the parade ground with full kit within only a few minutes, standing at attention without prompting.

Dupre and Lejaune stood in front of them, laughing between themselves, and then Lejaune addressed the gathered men.

'You foolish dogs! Do you really think that The Arabs would dare come to attack Sidi-Bel-Abbes? And do you think that we would turn to raw recruits like you if they did, men who have never even fired their rifles? You miserable sweepings of Europe's gutters! No. Today, you are going to learn to shoot. Corporal Dupre, go and inspect the caserne, if it is not clean, then the worst marksmen in this miserable collection of men will clean it all themselves'. Dupre ran off to inspect the barracks, as Lejaune continued.

'Now you scum, to the rifle range, forward, march! And sing! Sing, you dogs!'

The hundred or so men gathered in the barrack square began to sing 'Le Marseillaise' as they marched out towards the rifle-range, some two miles distant.

Mick, Dicken, Jimmy and Roumis easily mastered the rifled muskets, pot-marking their targets with accurate shots, as did most of the men, and for the first time, they heard Dupre and Lejaune actually praising them as they fired.

'Squeeze that trigger, don't pull it.'

'Well done lad, looks like you have a bullseye'.

It was as if the NCOs had finally gained a bit of respect for their charges as they could now shoot.

Most of the men were surprised that the musketry course lasted only a day, most of them firing no more than ten shots, but the new weapon was so advanced that it was easy to use. The reason given by their NCOs for the short duration of the musketry course was that Legionnaires rarely fired more than five or six volleys in an engagement, and that in the Legion's last big battle, in Europe at Magenta, they had fired just nine volleys. Besides, constant firing wasted ammunition. The next day, the men spent the morning practicing reloading, then the afternoon on bayonet drill. They then marched back to Sidi-Bel-Abbes for soup, bread and coffee, singing the new American ballad 'Lorena' on the way back:

"A hundred months have passed, Lorena
Since last I held that hand in mine
And felt the pulse beat fast, Lorena
Though mine beat faster far than thine
A hundred months ,'twas flowery May
When up the hilly slope we climbed
To watch the dying of the day
And hear the distant church bells chime.

We loved each other then, Lorena
More than we ever dared to tell
And what we might have been, Lorena
Had but our loving prospered well
But then, 'tis past, the years have gone
I'll not call up their shadowy forms
I'll say to them, Lost years, sleep on
Sleep on, nor heed life's pelting storms."

Back at Sidi, after eating, they were once again summoned onto the parade ground. There they were once more greeted by Captain Challier, the tall, barrel-chested officer who was supposed to be their CO, but whom they hadn't actually seen for many weeks. Challier spoke.

'My children, I am proud of you. France is proud of you. The Legion is proud of you. Your training is complete – you are now truly Legionnaires. Tomorrow, you will be divided up among the garrison companies here at Sidi-Bel-Abbes. I congratulate you mes enfants, your Emperor salutes you. Vive le France, and never forget our mottos – March or Die! - and Legio Patria Nostra!' (The legion is our homeland).

Those few words of encouragement from their hitherto mystical commanding officer in an instant blew away all the rage and resentment that the men felt about the weeks of seemingly monotonous training and hardship that they had endured. They were even more pleased when Lejaune spoke, after Challier had disappeared again.

'Legionnaires, fall out, be ready at reveille tomorrow with full kit – and bonne chance mes amis – good luck my friends.'

All at once, the Legionnaires saw the big picture. They had systematically been stripped of their own identity, even their own names, and reduced to little more than servile drones, but at the same time they had been shaped and moulded into soldiers, soldiers of the finest fighting force in the world, ready to take on a ferocious Arab enemy on his own ground, and beat him. They could march twenty miles a day on short water rations, they had the latest weapons and equipment, they had been physically aclimatised to one of the most difficult, challenging environments in the world, they had a splendid uniform and those who could not before now spoke enough of a foreign language, French, to use it in a combat situation. Challier, Lejaune and Dupre had given them a second chance, a chance to be soldiers – a chance to redeem themselves, an opportunity to be honourable once more - a chance to be heroes. They could also now perform battlefield manoeuvres, moving from column of fours, to twos, to firing line, to the dreaded square, and back to column of fours, quickly and almost without thinking, and to French orders.

The next morning after assembling in the barrack square, Mick, Jimmy, Roumis and Dicken were given splendid news that they had all prayed for – they were not to be split up. They were to join the 3rd Company, and report immediately for another intensive musketry course.

Chapter Fifteen– Jimmy Learns

The training was ghastly at first, Dicken had warned Mick and I about it, but even so, it was the hardest physical labour and test of endurance that I had ever had to suffer. We hardly ever saw our officer, Captain Challier, and the NCOs charged with turning us into soldiers seemed more intent on punishing us, either individually or collectively, for the most minor of infractions, than they did on turning us into proper Legionnaires. To be frank, I've never walked so much in my life as we did in those first few weeks. We marched, and we marched, and we marched. We did physical labour in and around Sidi-Bel-Abbes too, some of it worthwhile work, like improving fortifications or helping to repair roads, some of it little more than a tedious test of our character. For example, about a week into our training, Corporal Dupre and Sergeant Lejaune decided that a huge pile of mud bricks, thousands of them, needed to be moved to an almost identical location a mere fifty yards from where they had been dumped. Moving them served no purpose, but that was the point. We had to do it. We grumbled as we toiled in the baking hot desert sun, but the punishment given to one man who complained to the NCOs about the pointlessness of the allotted task deterred us from any other form of protest. To our surprise, it was none other than Roumis who made a remark to Dupre, astonishing, given that Dupre clearly had it in for Roumis from day one. We don't know what Roumis said to him – all we heard was Dupre calling out 'You insolent Arab dog!' before ordering Roumis to grab his rifle from where it had been piled along with ours, hold it above his head, and double-round the fortress 'until he dropped dead or caught le Cafard'.

Roumis did this unquestioningly. The perimeter of Sidi was very long, so every ten minutes or so, we would catch a glimpse of Roumis, rifle in the air, running round and round the fortress, his white-linen suit soaked with sweat. Roumis kept running, he didn't collapse, nor did he lose his discipline.

This seemed to annoy Dupre even more, but Roumis did exactly as he was told until the corporal decided that he had had enough of punishing Roumis for one day, ordering him to stop just as we ourselves had finished our rather pointless task with the bricks. Dupre didn't like Roumis at all, and made no secret of it, but he kept his niggling of our little Arab friend to an acceptable minimum, knowing that he was popular with many of the men, and grudgingly admiring the fact that Roumis rarely spoke back and seemed to learn quickly.

I often thought of Edinburgh, of my family, of the High Street and its sights and smells, but invariably such thoughts made me think about the reason that Mick and I had left Edinburgh, to sign away five years of our lives to serve in this ghastly, foreign, fiery furnace of a land. At no point did Mick or I even considering going on promenade though – we had joined The Legion for a fresh start and above all, to redeem our tarnished honour – not to run away again, not to desert.

Mick seemed to actually quite enjoy most of our training, even the tedious parts. He never seemed out of breath, seemed almost sedate under instruction, and he was never severely reprimanded or punished for anything, in fact, looking back, I thank my lucky stars that my Irish friend was there with me. He was the model soldier, I was just getting by. He would sometimes help me if I was going to be late for morning inspection, either by doing my share of cleaning the barracks where we slept, or by checking my kit for me. Dicken and Roumis were also great helps – we all looked after each other. Our training company contained many cliques at first, partly because of the language barrier. The German-speaking men tended to stick together, as did the French-speakers, though there was no hostility between us, and we even got to know our copains over Pinard some evenings, and would even sing with them. It was a source of great mirth to everyone that I had chosen 'Jimmy' as my nom de guerre and that Mick had chosen 'Mick' – us being Scottish and Irish, but the other men seldom asked questions about our background – such questions were actually considered extremely 'bad form' in The Legion, unless the man in question offered up such information voluntarily. We quickly learned that not everyone in The Legion was a fugitive from justice – far from it. Those who did speak of their pasts showed us that The Legion was quite the social mosaic –

indeed, a microcosm of European society – with Roumis as the 'joker in the pack'. Some of the men we trained with had joined up because they had been wounded in love, some had been kicked out of various European regular armies and were looking for a second chance in The Legion. Many had joined for purely economic reasons, to find a job, food, shelter and clothing, and some seemed to have joined up simply for the adventure. One man, a huge man from Alsace named Schwarz, had actually been a Major in Prussia's army, but had been forced to resign after fighting and winning a duel with another Prussian officer, who happened to be their Colonel's nephew. He too had sought a new life by starting at the bottom again, in The Legion. Of all the men of all the nationalities that we met, we never met a single man who had joined The Legion for the purpose of killing Arabs.

Ah Roumis. At first the other men that we trained with weren't happy at all about serving with an Arab – they barely trusted the Arab scouts or Goumier who worked for The French Armee d'Afrique (Army of Africa),let alone an Arab Legionnaire, but Roumis' local knowledge and his charming, friendly disposition soon won most of them over. Roumis knew where the safest places to go in Sidi-Bel-Abbes were, whether we were out to drink, to eat, to pursue women, or to do all three. His local knowledge was invaluable, particularly as it wasn't unheard of for Legionnaires to go missing or even be murdered when off duty.

Dicken too, was a great help. Not exactly a father figure, but like a big brother. His previous experience in The Legion often gave us an invaluable insight into just why we were doing certain tasks a certain way, day after day, week in, week out.

The training, almost all marching and kit maintenance at first, was monotonously dull, but the more we trained, the more adapt we became, the further we could march, the fitter we got. I put Mick's easier adaptation to Legion life than mine down to one simple fact – I had grown up and lived in smoky, smelly Edinburgh, a beautiful city but one which bred all sort of illnesses, whereas Mick had grown up on a farm near Sligo with plenty of fresh air.

Legion food, and our wine, or Pinard, was monotonous, but nutritious and fortifying, as long as we drank enough water to dilute the Pinard, and at least back at Sidi-Bel-Abbes, there was plenty to eat and drink. We were fed soup, bread and coffee two times a day. On the march, we were given hardtack biscuits – tasteless flour and water blocks that some said could actually stop bullets. Occasionally, the battalion charcutier would provide us with a special treat, usually some scraped pork chops or Boudin, a kind of blood sausage or black pudding, which when rolled up looked like a bit like the rolled up Legion blankets that topped our heavy backpacks on the march. We loved Boudin, it was our favourite food, a break from our monotonous diet. Only Roumis never touched it, because it was against his religion to eat the flesh of pigs, which in itself was a bonus – Mick and I usually got to eat his share.

Finally, after weeks of monotonous drill, cleaning and marching, we were led out one day to the rifle-range. All of our moods improved, as we were at last to undertake a task we deemed more befitting of a soldier. The basic musketry course lasted but one day, and every man passed. It wasn't exactly hard to hit targets with the rifled-musket, even those of us with little or no firearms experience could hit targets at 100 and 200 yards away with relative ease. Mick and Dicken were crack shots, Roumis wasn't that far behind them, and even I took to the beautiful weapon like a duck to water – though I did once fire my ramrod by mistake and was sent by a somewhat terse Sergeant Lejaune to retrieve it, much to the mirth of my comrades, whom Dupre had to tell to 'shut up' as they saw me trudging over to fetch it back from the firing range. I had went off at 'half-cock', but was sure that I would never make that mistake again.

The day after the rifle-range, we were given a morning's loading and reloading drill, then some bayonet drill, and then after being fed, we were told by Captain Challier on the parade ground that our training was completed, and that we were now proper Legionnaires! We were overjoyed. We were told that we had been assigned to the 3rd company of the garrison, and ordered to report on the parade ground the next morning with full-kit. Even Lejaune and Dupre seemed different that day, almost proud of us, but we were nevertheless glad to be leaving them behind, and felt sorry for the next poor batch of unfortunates who would have to train under them.

Chapter Sixteen– Mick Learns

I really enjoyed the training. I could tell Jimmy, Roumis and Dicken weren't so keen on it, but I loved it.

To me, it felt like a penance for all of the sins that I had committed before and since leaving Ireland, so every march, every sun-roasted day and every menial task felt to me like I was putting something back.

I loved being a soldier too. Jimmy and me got the best suits of clothes that we had ever owned, and in The Legion, no one ever bothered us about religion – we had left all that bigotry shite behind in Scotland. We were all Legionnaires. Most of the lads we trained with were decent enough fellas, though I did tend to hang around mostly with Jimmy, Roumis and Dicken. I did get a bit frustrated after a while, and I really felt like I needed to talk to someone about the past, Jimmy preferably, but there was little time for that. I picked up every skill and task easily, I kept my uniform clean, I never looked the NCOs in the face save for when they spoke to me, and I was even able to help Jimmy, as he seemed to struggle a little with some of the more minor tasks, mostly to do with cleaning and looking after his uniform. I put that down to his having lived a bit of a more comfortable life than I had, but that never made him a bad soldier.

I soon realised that Sergeant Lejaune and Corporal Dupre saw me as the model soldier. I thanked my lucky stars that neither of them was ever on my case about anything, but that was because I never gave them a single reason to be. In my whole time in Algeria, I never attended Mass once.

The food and drink we were served wasn't exactly gourmet, but at least there was plenty of it. Within a few weeks we could march twenty miles in a day on short water rations. We were encouraged to take particular care of our own and our comrades' feet, as bad feet on the march usually meant death for the Legionnaire concerned once on active service, either by the Arabs, or by thirst, after he had dropped out. We were told not to go back for stragglers, we were to 'march or die'.

When they finally let us fire our rifles instead of just marching about with them, I found that I was an excellent shot. I had seen British soldiers back in Ireland carrying rifled-muskets similar to our own, and now I knew why everyone seemed to have them. I knew that this new rifle would change war forever – it was far better than the rusty smoothbores that I had used back on the farm in Sligo. I missed Sligo, I thought a lot about Siobhan, my sister, but I didn't dwell on Ireland or on her too much, we were always so busy.

I loved going out on the town in Sidi-Bel-Abbes when we were paid. The women were beautiful, the locals friendly – as long as we weren't too drunk, and I even made a few bob on the side by taking on giant Arabs at bare-knuckle boxing. The lads would bet on me too, so we were all a few francs better off.

Time and again I would beat the living daylights out of some Arab giant in front of a small crowd, and time and again, I gave the astonished locals the reason for my victory – I was Irish!

The day after we finally went to the firing range, we did a little more drill, mostly bayonet practice, then our captain told us that our training was over and we were to report the next day with full kit to join the 3rd company. We were given a further, more intensive rifle course that morning, and then we went to meet our new officers and comrades from the 3rd company. Every man in our company was in for a bit of a shock.

Chapter Seventeen -March Or Die

The 3rd company of The Legion's Sidi-Bel-Abbes garrison was already waiting on the barrack square when Mick, Jimmy and the rest marched in and took up positions beside them. There were precisely eight men. Eight men. The new recruits weren't replacements for the new company, they were the new company. As soon as the 100 'new' Legionnaires joined the eight 'old hands' on the barrack square, there appeared in front of them a most unnerving sight. Four men, two officers and two NCOs, came and stood before the men, the corporal calling the stunned men to attention, before the senior officer spoke.

His uniform was immaculate, he had a big, strong chest like a barrel, and he wore the insignia of a headquarters, or staff, officer. It was Captain Challier! The two NCOs, both with outrageously large handlebar moustaches, and also wearing HQ insignia, were Corporal Dupre and Sergeant Lejaune!

No-one from the new men on the barrack square recognised the 4th man in front of them, but Challier soon clarified the whole situation.

'Legionnaires, I am the new commander of the 3rd company – your new commanding officer. I know most of you from basic training and I know that you will make good soldiers.'

He pointed to the eight, dust covered Legionnaires who had been on the barrack square when Jimmy, Mick and the rest had arrived, and continued speaking, whilst pointing.

'These eight brave men are all that is left of the old 3rd company. They were attacked four days ago by a mixture of Arab bandits while they were out escorting a topographical expedition some eighty miles south of Sidi, a few miles from El Abeid, an ancient deserted village that is the crossroads for dozens of caravans that cross the desert. Lieutenant Foster here and these eight men were the only survivors. They were attacked in the open by a bandit leader named Abdel-El-Krim, or just El Krim, and over 400 of his Berber and Touareg warriors. Our mission now is to be one of four infantry columns sent southwards towards El Abeid in order to locate and destroy this El

Krim. El Krim and his followers have challenged the honour of France, and of The Legion, by attacking us so close to Sidi, they are also the scourge of the peaceful Arab herdsmen and villagers. We will proceed to El Abeid as separate columns, but unite once we reach the ruined village, where our combined firepower will destroy these bastard camel-humpers. As our Emperor's uncle once said 'march divided, fight united', so we shall! The 1st, 2nd and 4th companies have already moved out and will scour the area to the west and east of El Abeid. Our duty is to recover the bodies of the men from the topographical mission, bury the bodies of our comrades, and bring back any weapons or kit that may have been left with their corpses. The Arab scouts will provide us with advance guards and flankers, and also keep us in touch with the other three companies en route. Now, Lieutenant Foster and I must attend on the Colonel, listen carefully to Sergeant Lejaune.

We march in half an hour, Vive La France!'

As Challier and Foster turned and made their way to the colonel's office, Lejaune took his turn to speak to the new company.

'During this march, you will remember our motto – March or die! You march, or you die. It is simple.

A word of advice now, keep one spare cartridge in your pocket, not for the enemy, but for yourself should you be faced with capture. These Arabs that we are after are like human wolves, who will think nothing of castrating and blinding a prisoner, before taking a week to torture him to death, they hate us, and this is their country, in their eyes. If you are captured, whatever you do, don't let them give you to the women. Better to attempt escape and be shot outright than be given to the women. Now, on this march, most of you will get your first taste of desert warfare – do not underestimate the enemy.

Just because they don't dress like us or fight like us, that doesn't mean that they're worse fighters than us, but, you are better soldiers. You have rifled muskets, you have bayonets, and above all, you have the honour of The Legion to uphold. Remember your training, mes amis, and all will be well.'

As Lejaune spoke, the assembled men's expressions changed again and again. Excitement, even delight on the faces of many when they were told that they would finally experience desert warfare, apprehension, but not fear, as Lejaune described the enemy, and pride, as they were reminded that they were trained Legionnaires. Lejaune finished his monologue in a sterner, more authoritative, gangster -like tone.

'Oh, I almost forgot. Listen carefully. I know that on this march, or during the coming fight, some of you will try to run away. Deserters will be shot out of hand. Desertion is not a solitary crime – every man who goes on promenade contributes to the weakening of the company, and thus increases the chances that his comrades will be killed. A deserter is like a knife in the back to his copain. And you won't get away. If the Arabs don't get you, the desert will. If the desert doesn't get you, The Legion will. If the Legion doesn't get you, I WILL.'

Not a man on the barrack square doubted a word that Lejaune had said.

Every man knew his duty. As soon as Challier and Foster returned from seeing the colonel, the 3rd company marched out of Sidi-Bel-Abbes, heading south, flanked by Arab scouts and with The Legion Flag and the Tricolour of France fluttering in the air overhead, Captain Challier mounted, the rest of the Legionnaires walking. It wasn't lost on Mick, Jimmy or any of the other men that they were being led by staff officers rather than front line officers, except for Lieutenant Foster, who had survived the 3rd company's last march to this destination. After a tedious, monotonous, uneventful four day march, during which they saw precisely zero enemy warriors, they reached the ruined village of El Abeid, four or five roofless mud brick, deserted buildings clustered around a well. The sight that greeted them there was like an Algerian version of Dante's Inferno…

Chapter Eighteen – Battlefield Detectives

Mick, Roumis, Jimmy and several other men from the 3rd company puked their guts out when they reached El Abeid's ruins. Dicken and the officers managed to contain their revulsion, but were still badly shaken. At a distance, at first, it had looked to them that El Abeid had already been reached by one of the other four companies. The Tricolour hung limp from the corner of one of the buildings, and blue coated Legionnaires appeared to be lazing around the tiny village in the hot sun. It was only when 3rd company got closer that they realised their error.

There were 127 bodies, mostly in Legion uniform, and they had been laid out in sitting or lying down positions post- mortem. Challier , still mounted, had uttered 'mon dieu' as he had clapped eyes on the grisly spectacle, and after assigning Dupre and Lejaune to post sentries and then carefully inspect the bodies, the two officers conferred together for a time, as the remainder of the company waited nervously in column of fours.

The hot air smelled utterly rank.

It smelled of death – blood, decaying flesh, gunpowder, rotten eggs, and of shit.

The smell of blood and of decaying, sun-scorched flesh was unmistakable, even to those among the company who had never smelled it before – it was the bodies of their dead fellow soldiers rotting in the hot African sun. The gunpowder and rotten egg smell indicated that a recent fire- fight had taken place, used black powder smelling almost exactly like spoiled egg. The smell of shit was from the bodies of those dead Legionnaires whose stomachs had been opened by their wounds, and also by natural faecal excretion that had occurred post-mortem in the victims, and been baked in the sun.

The tiny, deserted village was a scene of utter carnage. There had clearly been an attack on this isolated company, and they had evidently been overwhelmed, fighting hand-to-hand at the end, as none of the dead soldiers' bayonets were in their scabbards, and their rifles were nowhere to be seen. The Arabs hadn't stripped the Legionnaires of their uniforms, but had still mutilated the men almost beyond recognition. Instinctively, all of the 3rd company became aware that the uniforms must have been left on the dead Legionnaires by the Arabs for a reason, namely, to draw any would be rescuers into the same deadly trap!

The mutilations were terrible.

Men had been slashed from their genitals to their throats, others had had limbs cut off, some had been beheaded, and two soldiers were pinned to the walls of the mud-brick buildings with bayonets, and looked to have been castrated. 3rd company waited in silence, eerie silence, nervously scanning the horizon, trying not to breathe in through their noses. Asides the muttering of the two officers, the only sound to be heard was the true sound of death in the tropics.

Bzzzzzzzzzzzzzz.

Thousands of feeding insects had been sampling the prodigious feast offered by the Legion corpses.

The silence was then broken as, to most of the men's surprise, Lejaune called out 'ten minutes', indicating that the men could sit down and rest for the specified short time. Those men of the 3rd company who weren't posted as sentries sank to the ground, most of them falling clumsily backwards due to the sheer weight of the load that they carried, glad of the rest, but curious and wary about what would happen next.

'You, Englishman, come here' said Lejaune to Dicken, who sprang up as best he could, leaving his pack on the ground and walking over to where Dupre and Lejaune had joined the two officers in conversation, just out of earshot of the rest of the men. Mick and Jimmy saw Captain Challier hand a scrap of paper to Dicken, who read it, spoke briefly, then handed the piece of paper back to the captain, who in turn sent Dicken back to rejoin the men at the double, as the two officers and the NCOs continued speaking.

Mick spoke to Dicken first.

'Well, what's going on then? What the Hell's happened here?'

Dicken was still for a few seconds before replying.

'You, me, Jimmy and Roumis are to dig a big hole in the sand, now, come on, best hurry my friends. No dawdling.'

79

The four of them got out their shovels from their packs, stacked their rifles, and walked about twenty yards from the village, to a point where Dicken indicated that they should start to dig. There they began to dig what was obviously to be a mass grave for the other company. When the other Legionnaires saw what they were doing, they too piled their rifles and took up their trenching tools and helped to dig.

No-one ordered them not to help. As the soldiers dug and dug, the officers and NCOs continued talking to each other.

Lejaune and Dupre had surveyed the scene of the massacre and had found 124 dead soldiers, two dead white civilians and one dead Arab Scout. Challier and Foster had already noted that El Abeid should have been a safe defensive position – it had clear fields of fire on all four sides which would have afforded the company ample opportunity to mow down any attackers, and it even had a well, so they would not have had thirst as a consideration when conducting their defence. Moreover, apart from an escarpment to the south some 300 yards away where the desert terrain elevated slightly, any attack that the Arabs would have made would have been over open ground with no cover, meaning that a surprise attack had been extremely unlikely – if not impossible. Lejaune told the officers that he suspected treachery of some sort, and was asked to explain himself. Lejaune had noted that only one of the three Arab Scouts attached to the slaughtered company was accounted for. The company would have had three or four scouts, one on each flank, and another riding ahead of them, as was normal procedure. Yet only one Arab Scout's body was within the defensive perimeter. Challier, un-nerved, asked Lejaune to speak plainly.

'Captain, the Goum (scout) who died here was not shot by the Arabs, he was shot at point blank range in the back of the head, with a revolver, one of ours, judging by the wound. The company captain, lieutenants and NCO's were also killed in this manner, the same wound, with the same revolver, or at least the same model. The rest of the company were killed by musket balls or edged weapons. There are no Arab casualties on the field, no bodies at all. Muslims always bury the dead, even the enemy dead, unless they are in a hurry to escape or are planning some treachery. These bodies of our men have been left here deliberately, either to delay us, or to scare us. I think that one or two of the Arab Scouts were in fact spies for El Krim. I believe that they used their revolvers, which we gave them, to murder this poor company's leaders and the Arab Scout who had stayed loyal. Without leaders, the company would not have been able to conduct a coherent defence for very long, Sir. I think that we should bury our comrades and leave this place as soon as we have done so, one more thing sir – where are our own Goumier? Where are our own Arab Scouts?'

Challier was aghast, but remained cool.

'Thank you sergeant, your theory appears sound enough. There's no doubt that something sinister hindered the defence here. I agree, it's best that we bury our comrades and retreat a few miles, and wait to see if our own scouts return, or to see if the other two companies arrive safely. I see that it was the 1st company who fell. Sauzee's men.'

'Dear God' said Lieutenant Foster. 'So it was. Captain Sauzee always was a bit trusting, and vain, he has their company number stitched into the flag there.'

Sure enough, on the tricolour that was hanging on one of the walls, was stitched a simple '1' in the white bar.

'So sir, do we fall back?' Foster asked Challier, in his distinctive American accent.

Challier answered.

'Yes we shall, we have no choice, until our Goumier return we're as blind as bats and we're sitting ducks here, we will bury the dead and then-'

Chapter Nineteen– Les Arbis!

Captain Challier's head exploded, splattering blood and brain matter all over Foster, Dupre and Lejaune, a split second after a distant 'zip' had shattered the peaceful air and temporarily silenced the buzzing insects. A musket ball had smashed into the back of his head, the captain having been facing north at the time. As the lifeless corpse of the captain slumped out of his saddle and landed with a thud on the sand, Lieutenant Foster, Corporal Dupre and Sergeant Lejaune needed no further instructions.

Foster was now in command and simply said 'Aux Armes' to his two NCOs, who in turn bellowed the same order to the rest of the men, who had just finished digging the burial pit for 1st company.

With a mixture of fear and excitement, the Legionnaires rushed to snatch up their rifles, and Lejaune and Dupre set about positioning them in among the ruins of El Abeid, in among the remains of their fallen comrades, as the sentries came sprinting in from their posts to also take up positions among the more reassuring, if grisly looking, ruins, among their copains. Foster drew his sword and shouted orders to the two NCOs, who in turn relayed them to the men, and within minutes, the 3rd company had turned El Abeid into a deadly firing position. Poor Captain Challier's horse trotted in among the ruins too, and was tethered to the well. Mick, Jimmy, Roumis and Dicken were posted to the southern edge of the ruined village, alongside Foster himself, who peered through field glasses at the escarpment where the shot that had killed Challier had come from. All of the Legionnaires loaded their rifles, some with hands shaking, and fixed their bayonets, waiting. Trouble was surely coming their way, but they were at least ready for it, and eager to avenge fallen comrades.

Mick turned to Jimmy and gave him a wink, Jimmy smiled back at him. Roumis was motionless to their left, his rifle held as steady as a rock. Dicken was to Mick's right, nervously peering out to the south. Mick managed to whisper to him.

'So, what's the story here then Peter? What was on that bit of paper? And what happened here?'

At first Dicken didn't answer, then speaking like a true Legion veteran, he simply said 'You don't want to know, not right now. It'll be alright'.

Mick wasn't happy with the answer, neither was Jimmy, who heard the little exchange, but they trusted Dicken so they listened to his advice. Dicken added 'Do exactly what the lieutenant and NCOs say, and if they get popped, follow my lead. Just remember, we're Legionnaires, remember your training, it'll be alright.'

Though reassured, Mick and Jimmy were still a tad intrigued.

Just what had been on the piece of paper that the now-dead captain had asked Dicken to read?

And just who had fired the shot that had killed the captain?

All of the men now knew though that their own questions were irrelevant, and subordinate to the interests of The Legion, and of France. They had completed their apprenticeships, now it was time to get to work. C'est la Legion!

Chapter Twenty– Jimmy's Baptism

It was with apprehension rather than with excitement that I snatched up my rifled musket, as myself and the rest of the company dumped our trenching tools and took up our defensive positions in that tiny, ruined village called El Abeid. It was clear that our comrades in 1st company had been dead for less than 24 hours, the stench of their decaying corpses was almost unbearable. I was assigned to a section of the perimeter beside the man who was now leading us, Lieutenant Foster, the American, and I was relieved to be positioned beside Mick, Dicken and Roumis. We peered out into the desert, waiting, as Foster scanned the southward escarpment with his field glasses. We were ordered to load and to fix bayonets.

I admit it – my hands were shaking so badly that I dropped the first two percussion caps that I tried to place onto my rifle's nipple, before I finally got the third one on. I looked around. Mick looked almost excited, eager, like a big boy playing soldiers. Dicken was his usual quiet self, saying nothing, as still and calm as a man on a firing range back at Sidi. Roumis too, was like a statue, his bayonet tipped rifle pointing out into the desert. We waited, and waited. Then we saw five camels with riders move down from the escarpment, out of the haze, towards us.

The camels weren't exactly moving very quickly and their riders weren't brandishing swords or carrying rifles, in fact, they sat bolt upright on their mounts, hardly moving, as their camels slowly brought them towards us. They were clearly Arabs, judging by the way they were dressed. We wondered if they were performing some sort of suicide charge to inspire their hidden comrades, if there were any, which there had to be, unless it was one of these five camel riders who had shot our captain dead.

On they came and still they made no sound nor produced any weapons, they didn't show any fear, though their faces were hidden by their robes anyway. Lieutenant Foster put away his field glasses and drew his revolver, then shouted to Sergeant Lejaune in French that the north, east and west sides of our tiny perimeter were to stand fast and keep looking ahead, orders which were quickly relayed to the men by Lejaune and Dupre. Meanwhile, the four of us, the lieutenant, and the other twenty men in our company who were facing south, received our orders from Foster.

When the camel riders got to within 100 yards of us, to my surprise, rather than order a volley, Foster called out to Dicken, in English, telling him to fire at the camel-rider on the far left of the five camel squadron that was approaching. Dicken aimed, squeezed the trigger, and a split second later his rifle sent a minie bullet smashing into the rider's head, causing what looked like a little puff of red smoke as the blood in the man's head was splattered into the air. Foster told Dicken to reload.

The other four camel riders seemed completely unbothered by Dicken's shot, and continued towards us.

When they got to 50 yards range, Foster ordered us to fire a volley at them, and then to reload.

An almighty crash resounded as 24 rifles went off together, blasting all but one of the remaining Arabs from their mounts, and even the one who remained on his camel was hit at least twice. The three who were blasted from the saddle were literally torn apart – I think one of them was hit by ten bullets.

Still, they had not made any attempt to fire on us or to spur their mounts forward. Foster gave no further order to fire, and when the last camel and rider were within ten yards of our position, Foster sent Mick and Dicken to tackle him, though all the while, the rider had 24 rifles aimed at him at point blank range.

The Arab on the back of the camel was still upright, but didn't move, though blood stains saturated his robe. Dicken managed to slide the man off his camel and bundled him onto the ground.

Foster called out to Roumis to help Mick secure the camel, which Roumis sprinted out to do, but the beast was docile enough, and just stood still, oblivious, and remarkably, unhurt. Such was the accuracy of our wonderful rifled muskets.

The lieutenant then tore off the dying Arab's robes, with Dicken's help. What they saw when they removed his robes clearly un-nerved them both, Foster vomiting while Dicken did his trademark wipe of his forehead with his hand, which was usually about as much agitation as he ever showed to anything, but even at that, soon all of us knew why those five camel riders hadn't made any attempt to charge or to fight, and this knowledge told us that we were soon to be in for the fight of our lives.

Chapter Twenty-One – Greek Tragedy

Lieutenant Foster and Dicken's investigation of the downed camel-rider at last gave 3rd company an insight into what had happened at El Abeid. The man in Arab robes was in fact a captured Legionnaire, a white man- but he was no turncoat. His eyes had been put out, to blind him. His tongue had been cut-out of his head, to stop him from speaking. His arms had been broken in several places, and he had a wooden rod up his back to keep him upright and strapped to the Camel. Upon seeing this, Foster sent Dicken, Mick and Roumis to investigate the other four 'Arabs' who had fallen onto the sand, then the Lieutenant shouted for Sergeant Lejaune and Corporal Dupre to join him.

The officer and the two NCOs spoke for a few minutes, and then Foster shot the poor, blinded, dying man in the head with his pistol, ending his misery.

Dicken, Mick and Roumis, having inspected the other four bodies, carried one of them over to where Foster, the NCOs and the dead 'Arab' were, a few yards from the ruins. Dicken quickly reported that the man they had brought over was still alive. Like the other four men, he had been blinded, had his tongue cut out and had been badly disjointed, but he was still alive, and appeared to have been knocked from the saddle by a single minie ball to the shoulder. He wasn't a Legionnaire though, he really was an Arab.

Lieutenant Foster didn't speak Arabic; only Roumis did, so Foster asked Roumis to talk to the man, who seemed near delirious. Blood still poured from where the poor Arab's eyes had been, and his mouth and chin were covered in blood from when his tongue had been cut out. Dicken was told to help Roumis to question the dying man as best he could, which would involve Roumis whispering to the man, who was clearly the loyal one of 1st company's Arab Scouts, and the blind man writing down his answers as best he could in Arabic. Roumis tried to give the poor man some water before they began, but Dicken stopped him, telling Roumis that they would give him a drink afterwards.

Roumis asked the man several questions, in a soft but urgent voice, as he stroked the man's hair.

The man, though horribly mutilated, blinded and dying, knew exactly what was expected of him, and began to write on the back of the same piece of paper that Dicken had been asked to read earlier.

Almost immediately, Roumis protested to the dying man in Arabic, but by now the Scout was writing of his own free will, albeit rather messily, but still rather well for a blind man.

Dicken told Roumis to stop reprimanding the man for what he was writing, so he did. Just as the scout finished writing on the scrap of paper, Dicken finally let him drink some water. Despite his eyes and tongue being gone, despite his multiple wounds, the scout smiled as he sipped the water, and then fell forever silent.

Dicken snatched the piece of paper that the scout had been writing on, looked at it, and then relayed its contents to Foster and the NCOs. After that, Dicken, Mick, and Roumis were sent to rejoin their comrades while the lieutenant, sergeant and corporal spoke to each other.

There was still no sign of 3rd company's own scouts, nor of any enemy activity from the direction of the southward escarpment.

Chapter Twenty-Two –Mick's Baptism

I tell you, I've seen some horrible sights in my life, but what those bastard Arab bandits did to our boys was like something straight of that book by Dante that Mr. Graves used to show us back in Sligo, but worse! They had taken one of our loyal scouts, and four of our Legionnaire comrades that they had captured, and strapped them to camels, dressed up like Arabs, but blinded and with their tongues cut out, and their arms broken. I thought that they had done this purely out of barbarism, but Dicken explained everything to us when we got back into the ruins at El Abeid.

Their tongues had been cut from their heads to prevent them from shouting 'don't shoot' at us as their camels were basically aimed at our position and encouraged forward.

Their eyes had been cut out so that they couldn't see what they were riding towards, as they still had their ears, the Arabs could have told them just to ride in our direction, perhaps assuring them that they would be set free if they did.

Their arms had been broken to stop them from turning the camels away from the course that the Arabs had set them on – towards us, and they had been dressed as Arab bandits so that we would open fire on them. The one eventuality that the Arabs hadn't allowed for was for one of the doomed camel-riders to make it to our lines alive and able to write, and that's where Dicken had come in useful.

Though Roumis and the blinded Arab Scout could have a one-way conversation in Arabic, it turned out that the now dead, blinded scout could speak and understand Arabic and Greek, but could only write in Greek. Useless to Roumis, but Dicken knew Greek from his school days!

Full of surprises, that was our Peter Dicken. The scout, called Ahmed, had been born and raised in Egypt, and had been an Ottoman Bashi-Bazuk there and in The Sudan as a young man, and being raised in Egypt, that's how he could write in Greek.

Dicken then told us what the scout had written on that piece of paper, and on the other piece he had been shown earlier by Captain Challier, which had been a general warning in Greek, warning any

89

solitary Legion companies not to linger at El Abeid because it was a trap. That El Krim fella, the Arab bandit leader, had nearly a thousand warriors, many more than we or our officers had thought. He had also managed to plant an agent at Sidi, who ended up assigned to 1st company as a scout, and whose job it had been to kill all of 1st company's officers and NCOs as soon as El Krim had them surrounded.

The rogue scout was also to kill the loyal scouts, but one of them had gotten away just before 1st company was encircled, riding hell for leather to the north to fetch help, not from the other companies, but from Sidi itself, just as the now deceased Captain Sauzee had ordered him to do so in the case of any unexpected developments. Ahmed hadn't been so lucky, and had been kept alive and tortured after the Arabs had over-run 1st company, as El Krim hoped to find out if his plan of drawing some of the Legion into a trap was going to work. El Krim hoped to destroy a full battalion of The Legion in order to bring more local Arab tribes over to his side, and eventually to raise an army big enough to drive us 'hated infidels' back into the Mediterranean Sea. Who'd have thought that two scribbled notes in Greek written by an Egyptian scout and read by an Englishman, in order to try to save foreign soldiers fighting for France, could have had such importance? When I asked Dicken why he had never mentioned anything in the first note to us, he simply said that he had been asked not to until the situation became clearer. Dicken was a dark horse, but a faithful one. I found myself wondering what other hidden talents he might have had.

Maybe he could fly? He didn't laugh when I cracked that joke.

Anyways, Dicken being able to read Greek had clarified our situation; it did nothing to improve it.

We now knew that there were odds of at least 10-1 against us here at El Abeid, unless the other two companies arrived soon. Lieutenant Foster made Lejaune tell the company a shorter, summarised version of what was going on, which at least let the rest of the boys know how things stood. We were outnumbered 10-1, unsure of when relief was coming, and of course, El Krim's Arabs now had over 100 of our rifled muskets, taken from the bodies of 1st company. Ten minutes after Lejaune's briefing, our own three Arab scouts arrived at El Abeid, shaken and wounded, but otherwise okay. No sooner had they arrived and watered their horses than Lieutenant Foster sent them out again, one to the north to get help from Sidi, the others to the east and the west to warn the other companies of what was going on. We assumed that the other, unaccounted for scout who had been attached to 1st company had indeed rode for Sidi, in which case, we might get relief sooner than if we waited for our own company's scout to complete that mission. Lieutenant Foster also told them not to return to El Abeid without help, as it was more important that The Legion knew the bigger strategic picture; our little company was expendable.

Did that mean that we were going to lie down and let ourselves be ridden down like 1st company?

Did it hell!

We had our officer, and our two NCOs, we had our rifles, bayonets and plenty of ammunition. We had no intention of being beaten by amateur tribesmen. Bloody camel-humpers!

We were given the order to drink by Dupre, and we did, one cup, as ever. Then just as we had all finished screwing the lids back onto our water bottles, we heard a volley of shots ring out from the south, and we heard hundreds of bullets zipping harmlessly high over the ruins of El Abeid, then we heard a huge roar coming from the southern escarpment, and looking to the south, we saw a dust cloud. I looked at Jimmy as we all rushed back into our positions within the ruins, and asked him if he was alright. He looked startled but he simply said 'C'est la Legion!'

We both laughed, and then our training kicked in as our NCOs began to bark orders at us. Foster stood as cool as a cucumber, arms folded, watching El Krim's men as they made their battle formation.

We were outnumbered, but we were professionals, we were Legionnaires, and we were ready for them. Arab drums started to beat, a slow war tap, it was clearly designed to scare the shite out of us, but it did nothing of the sort – we were more scared of Lejaune and Dupre than we could ever be of El Krim's men. Then the Arabs charged…

Chapter Twenty-Three - The Oldest Trick

Lieutenant Foster strode among his men with a confident swagger, revolver in hand, the epitome of coolness, as the men of 3rd company watched the vast horde of Arab warriors that were advancing to El Abeid. This lot had already almost annihilated 3rd company in the open a few days before, Foster and a tiny handful of men being the only escapees, but here was the 3rd company ready to face the same enemy once more. Lieutenant Foster shouted 'camel humpers!', and all of the Legionnaires who waited in their firing positions laughed aloud. At first the mass of Arabs to the south had been almost invisible to the Legionnaires because of their own dust cloud and the desert haze, but that soon changed.

3rd company was met with the sight of nearly a thousand Arabs charging towards them, some on horses, some on camels, some on foot, no two warriors dressed the same. They brandished muskets, swords, lances, pistols and some even had what looked like farming implements. They also carried several banners emblazoned with Koranic slogans. If it had not been for the presence of firearms in their ranks, they could just as well have been Mohammed's army from the early days of Islam. They were a quasi-feudal force set on attacking and destroying another company of the accursed infidel soldiers, the hated 'Roumis'. That was neither here nor there to the Legionnaires though, to them, this was their baptism, and to their officer, it was a matter of revenge.

The Legionnaires waited as still as statues, still deployed on all four sides of the ruined village, despite the fact that the Arabs were attacking only from the south.

Then, when the charging mass of warriors got to within 200 yards of the ruins, Foster gave the order to fire, and the twenty-odd rifled-muskets on the south side of the defences spluttered out a deadly volley, staggering the Arab advance but not halting it.

Foster then shouted orders in French, instructing the men manning the other three sides of the ruins to join their comrades on the south side, so that a full company volley could be delivered into the Arab mass.

'Shoot the mounted ones, the ones carrying flags, and any of them who are trying to shoot back' roared Foster, in his broad American-French accent.

Dupre and Lejaune soon had the whole company pouring rapid volleys into the Arabs, one half of the company firing, while the others reloaded, and by the time the Arab line reached 50 yards of El Abeid, the men in the line were having to climb over dead Arabs, horses and camels in order to continue advancing upon the Legionnaires. A final volley from the Legionnaires flattened what was left of the Arab front ranks, and then, with a massed shriek of terror, the huge Arab force, which had lost over 100 men, lost its nerve and turned to run away, many dropping their weapons. The Legionnaires had lost only two men to enemy fire.

Lieutenant Foster roared an order to reload, which most of the men did, apart from the two platoons on the extreme left.

To Foster's exasperation, he turned to see that Sergeant Lejaune and Corporal Dupre had led two platoons, about forty men, in a bayonet charge to pursue the retreating Arabs towards the escarpment. The two platoons sprinted after the fleeing Arabs, bayoneting wounded Arabs as they passed them and firing into the backs of those Arabs who had run away. Mick, Dicken, Roumis and Jimmy and the rest of 3rd company who had remained in their positions gave a loud cheer, and fully expected Foster to lead them forward in support, but Dupre and Lejaune's men were now a good 200 yards from El Abeid, and Foster roared the order for the men left at El Abeid to stand fast. The Legionnaires had repulsed El Krim's men easily- a bit too easily.

To the horror of Foster and of the men in El Abeid, the Arab retreat had been a clever trick, a feigned retreat, a tactic as old as warfare itself, designed to draw all, or some, of the enemy out from the safety of his fortified position and into the open. Lieutenant Foster was too experienced to have fallen for that trick, but Lejaune and Dupre had been rash, and now they and their forty Legionnaires were cut off out in the open. The Arabs were no soft touches.

Hundreds of mounted Arabs, who had only moments earlier been retreating, now turned around to quickly encircle Lejaune and Dupre's little band, many of whom had not even had a chance to reload their rifles. Lejaune did his best to get them into a square formation to repulse the Arabs, but it was too late. With point blank gunfire, sword slashes and lance thrusts, Lejaune and Dupre's command was quickly wiped out. They lost their cohesion in the open, and in spite of gallant resistance, they were all soon lying sprawled in the dust among the jubilant swarm of Arabs, being hacked to pieces.

The remaining 70 or so men at El Abeid under Foster had been waiting for the lieutenant to order them forwards to help their comrades.

The order never came.

Foster even threatened three Legionnaires with his revolver when they tried to leave the relative safety of El Abeid to join Lejaune's doomed command.

Foster knew what was coming next.

As the whole Arab force once again began to advance towards El Abeid, this time they fanned out in an encircling manoeuvre, obviously planning to wipe out 3rd company, again, albeit in a different location. When the charge came, it was loud, terrifying and intense. And the Legionnaires were ready for it.

Mick spoke briefly to Dicken, as the men at El Abeid were dispersed to man the whole perimeter once more.

'Why didn't Foster let us go and help those boys?'

Dicken answered straight away, without averting his glance from the approaching enemy.

'Throwing good men after bad, so to speak, my friend. Lejaune messed that up there, if we'd charged into the open to help them we'd all be hacked to pieces too by now. Foster had to preserve enough men to man the perimeter here, that took discipline. Trust me; we'll thank him for that later. If we get out of here.'

70 rifles and one revolver was not sufficient firepower to defend the ruined village against 800 Arabs, Foster knew that, but he also knew that they stood a better chance of survival defending the ruins and the precious well than they did in the open. As the Arab circle closed around the village, Foster ordered the men to begin independent fire as soon as the Arabs got to within 150 yards. Hardly a shot missed. Each rifled musket leveled at an Arab and fired

resulted in a kill, and for almost two hours, Mick, Dicken, Roumis, and Jimmy loaded and fired, loaded and fired, making a great slaughter of the Arab force.

Foster, and indeed some of the Legionnaires, realised that as soon as the Arabs opted for encirclement, they would have to stop using their own firearms and resort to cold-steel only, in case they hit their own men. This evened things up a little and kept El Krim's men at a distance. Lieutenant Foster had turned what had been an embarrassing reverse into a favourable stalemate, particularly if the Arabs were relying on water from El Abeid's well - the very centre of 3rd company's position. That would only be a useful situation for as long as the Legionnaires' ammunition lasted, and after nearly two hours of repeated attacks, it was almost all gone.

Chapter Twenty-Four –

Jimmy's Beautiful Terror

That first Arab attack truly was a baptism of fire for me, Mick, Roumis and most of the lads. Foster and Dicken had did it all before, but I think that even they were un-nerved by this particular action. At first we were jubilant when the first Arab attack faltered and retreated after only a few volleys from us, my, I have to say, what a fine weapon the rifled-musket was. Even in the hands of recently trained marksmen like us, it was deadly. Perhaps the easiness with which we repulsed the first attack was what drove Lejaune to lead nearly half of the men out of the line and into pursuit of the fleeing Arabs. Foster shouted after him to recall his men, but on they rushed, straight into the trap that El Krim had set for them.

I knew instinctively why Foster hadn't allowed anyone else to try to rescue Lejaune's command, and Dicken explained why to Mick when he asked. It was truly horrible having to helplessly watch our comrades being butchered, made even worse by the fact that once the Arabs had encircled their tiny, hastily assembled square, we ourselves couldn't even give them fire support. We had little time to grieve.

As soon as The Arabs had wiped out Lejaune's command, they again came back at us, this time encircling us from all sides. It was hot work, damned hot work, but under the brave Lieutenant Foster's command, we kept up a withering independent fire for the best part of two hours, which kept the Arabs at bay.

I was scared, we all were, but we were also exhilarated. All of our training was paying off, and the ground around El Abeid was littered with dead enemy warriors, smashed to pieces by the high velocity slugs from our rifled muskets. Foster had long since expended his pistol ammunition, and was now fighting with a bayonet-less rifle taken from one of our two casualties. We were down to three rounds a man by early evening, and fully expected to be over-run, and then to add to our increasingly desperate plight, we heard some sort of horns or trumpets in the distance, and we saw another dust cloud to the south. More Arab horsemen, we deduced.

Mick, Dicken, Roumis and I all looked at each other, betraying no real emotion outwardly, simply giving each other a goodbye nod of the head, as the Arab circle around us prepared for the charge that would finally ride us down. We all reloaded and waited, and brought our rifles back to our shoulders as again we heard trumpets, a drum, and the unmistakable sound of massed horses' hooves – the final charge was coming!

Chapter Twenty-Five - Mick's Relief

About 600 additional horsemen had entered the battle, from the escarpment to the south, and they thundered towards our tiny, beleaguered position. Their swords hacked and slashed, cutting men in two, and they charged knee to knee straight for us – killing everything in their path.

The horsemen who had entered the fray were our own cavalry, that is to say, the red and blue uniformed cavalrymen of France's Chasseurs d'Afrique. They rode down all of the Arabs who had been on our southern side, then as they reached the ruins we were by now cowering in, they split into two battalions, each wheeling off to destroy the Arab forces to our east and west, smashing through the enemy like a hammer breaking glass, their sabres glinting in the fiery African sun. The Arabs, who had minutes earlier been on the verge of a great victory, now found themselves helpless as the Chasseurs d'Afrique caught them in the open, in much the same way that Lejaune's men had been caught in the open a few hours earlier. We were also pleased to see what looked like the missing Arab loyal scouts riding in front of the Chasseurs d'Afrique, slashing away at El Krim's men with their own swords, having guided France's cavalry across the desert to our rescue. We later found out that only one Arab scout had been an enemy agent, and one of the Chasseurs had split him in two with his sabre at the start of the engagement, after one of our loyal scouts had pointed him out.

With the southern approach cleared, and the east and west approaches also being quickly cleared by the Chasseurs d'Afrique, that left only one quarter of the Arab force still intact, the one to our north. I was then amazed when Lieutenant Foster ordered us to charge our bayonets and rush towards the Arabs to the north – amazed but oh so proud!

Shoulder to shoulder with Dicken, Jimmy and Roumis, and the rest of what was left of our company, we rushed towards the two hundred or so other Arabs to our north, making as much noise as possible, Lieutenant Foster now brandishing his sword and yelling 'come on boys!'.

There was one Arab in that group who looked different from the rest. Dressed head to toe in red and black and with strange headgear, he was surrounded by what looked like ten bodyguards – the only warriors in the Arab force who were dressed uniformly .Foster seemed to know who he was : it was El Krim.

El Krim's men fired a useless volley at us which sailed high over our heads, and that was our signal to return fire. Foster told us to aim for the bodyguards, and at only 150 yards, we couldn't really miss, and all their saddles were soon empty, apart from El Krim's. He tried to rally the other 200 or so men around him, but they were beginning to break, they weren't trained to fight defensive actions, it wasn't in their nature, and it showed. They hesitated for about a minute as we reloaded and marched a few paces forward. Now it was they who were intimidated! So intimidated, in fact, that they went down like sheep, as both battalions of the Chasseurs d'Afrique slammed into their flanks, fresh from slaughtering the Arabs on the other flanks and putting to flight the handful who had survived.

Then, without orders, Roumis leveled his rifle and shot El Krim's horse out from under him, meaning the Arab leader would be hacked to pieces by the Chasseurs d'Afrique, along with all of his men who stayed to fight. Our cavalry made short work of that lot too, and then, just to crown it all, we heard a familiar bugle call, and to our left, we saw two Legion companies sprinting up towards us, rifles at the trail, it was the 2nd and 4th companies, our long expected relief!

Better late than never.

I turned to shake hands with the boys, we were all so exhilarated. We had been on the verge of defeat, of certain death, but our cavalry's timely intervention had saved the day, and presumably ended this El Krim's nonsense forever – though I did hear that he had a son.

The Arab bandits were totally destroyed; our only regret was the loss of Captain Challier, and of Lejaune and his two platoons.

Lieutenant Foster spoke to the Chasseurs' colonel for a time after the battle, and it was explained to us that our scouts had indeed saved us, by riding off for help, and crucially had, by sheer chance, encountered our cavalry – The Chasseurs d'Afrique - on the ride north and persuaded them to come to our aid at El Abeid. The infantry relief later sent from Sidi would have arrived too late to save us, but our cavalry had arrived in the nick of time, just by virtue of the fact that they had happened to be on patrol a few miles to our north-east when they encountered the scouts. We had repelled the most monstrous enemy force, and only a few of us were dead. We were ordered back to Sidi-Bel-Abbes right away, while 2nd and 4th companies were detailed to bury the dead, both at El Abeid and nearby where the 'old' 3rd company had been defeated a few days earlier, and to tend to the wounded. The Chasseurs d'Afrique went charging off over the horizon, in pursuit of any fugitives from El Krim's force.

Wounded Arabs were shot or bayoneted where they lay– C'est la Legion – we could have expected no better from them if the roles had been reversed.

Our five-day march back to Sidi was as uneventful as we could hope for. We hardly saw a soul, other than when we passed our own relief column from Sidi, and they just continued south, intending to mop up any Arab resistance, and with orders to tear down the buildings at El Abeid.

I was glad that Dicken, Roumis and Jimmy were unhurt.

When we got back, Lieutenant Foster was soon promoted to Captain for his heroic actions at El Abeid.

That pleased us.

Jimmy found time to send a letter home to his parents in Edinburgh, just to let them know that he was okay and was still alive. I also took up the pen, writing to a family who I knew back in Sligo, to hopefully have news passed to my sister, Siobhan, that I was alright. Neither of us divulged what we were doing for a living now, though both of us were careful to mention that we were writing from Sidi-bel-Abbes, so that it wouldn't take much for our families to figure out what had become of us. We were still fugitives from the law in Britain and Ireland, but we were untouchable in The Legion. Neither of us received a reply the whole time that we were back at Sidi.

For a time it was rumoured that the entire Legion was going to be sent to North America, to fight on the side of the Confederates in America's civil war, but all talk of that ceased by October 1862, when we learned that the Confederate Army had been defeated in an almighty battle at Antietam, a victory for the Union side which quickly led to their President abolishing slavery in the United States forever.

That put an end to any chance we had of being sent to that war, as neither France nor Britain was ever going to side with the Confederates, who still fervently supported the reviled institution of slavery.

One day I checked a calendar at Sidi, late October, 1862. Talk all over the fortress then was of a new war, far away across the Atlantic, France's Imperial Regular Army having recently been defeated at a place called Puebla in Mexico, after France had taken a 'side' in Mexico's civil war, or something like that.

The talk wasn't of the war itself, but of why The Army and France's Emperor, Napoleon III, nephew of Napoleon Bonaparte, had decided that The Legion would not be involved in Mexico. Most of us were hurt by that, not least because the regular army had been defeated, and we now wanted a chance to prove that we were better than them.

In the later months of 1862, we didn't do much soldiering, it was back to drill, cleaning and manual labour, but all the while we griped to our NCOs about being excluded from this Mexican adventure.

They themselves weren't exactly pleased to be left out either, so they in turn, griped to the captains, who griped to the senior officers, who griped to our generals, who then sneakily went over the Regular Army's head and directly petitioned Napoleon III to send The Legion to Mexico. The army was said to be incensed by this, but Napoleon gave in, and in late 1862 we were told that we would be sailing to Mexico just after New-Year. We were excited!

We were a little deflated when we found out that only 1500 Legionnaires would be sent – two fighting battalions, a staff and headquarters company, a small medical unit and a big marching band. To the relief of me, Jimmy , Roumis and Dicken, we were among those troops selected to go to Mexico, as part of the 3rd company of the new 1st battalion – the superstitious among us were glad that we were still 'number 3' company. We sailed from Oran on the 9th of February 1863, and arrived in the stinking port of Vera

Cruz in Mexico on March 28th. The seven week voyage was pleasant enough, if a little tedious, but we did have plenty of time to finally have a talk whilst at sea. Captain Foster had a lot of time for us, and us for him, and on the way to Mexico, we talked about many things, including Foster's past, hitherto unknown, and the reasons why France was fighting, and losing, a war in Mexico. That took us a while to get our heads around.

Chapter Twenty-Six – Vamos A Mexico

The Legion's pleasant, if a little tedious, Atlantic crossing gave the men in the newly formed companies time to rest physically, and to get to know each other a little better. The newly-promoted Captain Foster chose to travel with his men rather than on a ship that was 'officers only', and the men of 3rd company admired him for that. The fact that Foster was American seemed to give them added confidence in him, even though it was to Mexico, not the United States, that they were sailing. One night, as the men drank pinard and smoked cigars, the usually quiet Dicken asked Captain Foster just how he had come to be an officer in French service, and Foster answered with a quite straightforward, yet compelling story.

'Well you see boys, I am from New Orleans in Louisiana. My wife was French, and I was educated at West Point in the 1840's. I was a captain in the US Army, stationed at a God-forsaken outpost in Missouri. I was miserable without my wife, Anna, and asides a few skirmishes with Indians, the life was boring, but tolerable. The argument over slavery which has now erupted into full-blown war back in my homeland was back then, still just an argument. Then in 1857, President Buchanan decided to try to divert the country's attention from the slavery issue to the Mormon issue. Mormons are a sort of new Christian people who had been persecuted by several states in the past, and had thus chosen to move en masse to the desert of Utah, where they had set up their own state legislature and built a great city in the desert beside the Great Salt Lake. Back east, nearly everybody hated the Mormons, chiefly because some of them openly practiced polygamy, and also because their state government was also their church leaders. They chased federal officials out of Utah and even talked openly about being independent from the United States. President Buchanan saw them as ideal scapegoats to divert attention from the slavery issue, so he did something that no American ever thought would be done – he sent out a US Army against US Citizens. 2500 of us were sent westward to Utah. We were actually only being sent to re-assert federal authority, but the Mormons misinterpreted our intentions, and thought we were coming to wipe them off the face of the earth. Because of this misunderstanding, a caravan of innocent American pioneers, whose wagon train just happened to be crossing Mormon territory at the same time as our advance, was massacred by a combined force of Mormon militia and Paiute Indians at a place called Mountain Meadows. Around 130 unarmed men, women and children were butchered in cold blood by the Mormons and the Indians. My patrol found them and buried them not long afterwards, as they had been buried in shallow graves, it was sickening. We erected a memorial on the spot, a simple wooden one on which we wrote 'vengeance is mine, sayeth the lord'.

We later heard that the Mormon leader later destroyed our memorial. The Mormons blamed the entire incident on their Paiute allies. In the end, our little 'war' with the Mormons ended before it really began – the massacre I told you about quickly forced the Mormons to make some concessions to the federal government, so we were withdrawn. I actually had some sympathy for the Mormons before Mountain Meadows, they only wanted to be left alone in the desert, but teaming up with Indians against whites was just too bad. Many of the men in my company had wanted to raze the Mormon's city to the ground – but that's not what I joined the army for. As we trudged back eastwards towards winter quarters, I feigned illness and was transferred to a hospital wagon, and my lieutenant was given command of the company. So, knowing that my men weren't leaderless, and also knowing that the failure of our Mormon expedition meant that the next war that the US Army fought would be a civil war over slavery, I went on promenade, or as we said in the US Army, I took 'the grand bounce' – I deserted. I had no desire to fight against fellow Americans, that's not why I joined the army.'

'So, then what did you do, sir?' asked Dicken.

'I rode as fast as I could for the Mississippi, and took a boat to New Orleans, where to my horror, I discovered that my wife Anna had died in a Yellow Fever epidemic. We had no children, and I was a fugitive from the army, so at New Orleans I said goodbye to the land of the free and took ship to France. I went to stay with Anna's family in Bordeaux for a time, and as her uncle was secretary to France's Minister for War, he was able to get me a 2nd lieutenant's commission in The Legion, for the price of a few modest but well directed bribes. I didn't change my name, as I wanted to redeem my honour. I was promoted to 1st lieutenant for bravery under fire at Magenta against the Austrians in 1859, and after that, I was sent to North Africa.'

'What was the brave deed that you did, sir?' asked Jimmy.

'It was nothing really. I ran back to save our wounded colour-bearer, his legs had been shattered by a cannon-ball. It didn't do him any good sadly; he died of an infection three years later. Every night when I sleep, I see his face, pleading with me to shoot him and end his suffering rather than save him. Sometimes I wish I had'. Foster then stared into space momentarily.

Dicken then spoke.

'Seems that many of us have joined The Legion to either escape something, or to save our honour, or both'.

'C'est la Legion' said Foster.

Mick then spoke.

'So, sir, this big civil war that's goin' on in America right now, what side would you have chosen?'

Foster was silent for a moment, then spoke, like an enthusiastic schoolteacher.

'Well boys, my state, Louisiana, is on the Confederate side. The Confederates claim that they are fighting for independence, for state's rights, and for their freedom. I agree with that in principal. However boys, they're hypocrites. They claim to be fighting for freedom, yet they are really fighting for the freedom to maintain the institution of slavery. I don't get that. How can men say they fight for freedom, while they deny it to others, to a whole race of men? For that reason and that reason alone, I'd have stayed in the US Army and fought for The Union and to free the slaves.'

Captain Foster was taken aback when the group of Legionnaires who had been listening to his tale began clapping. Then he spoke to Mick.

'Don't you ever have any doubts, Mick?'

Mick knew exactly what Foster was talking about, and answered honestly.

'Of course I do, sir. I'm Irish, my country has been invaded and colonised by foreigners for hundreds of years, when I realised that France was doing exactly that in North Africa, and that I was going to have to help to do that, I felt like a bit of a hypocrite, sir. But sir, The Legion has given me and Jimmy here a second chance, and believe me, any sympathy that I had for the Arabs vanished when I saw the dead, mutilated bodies of 1st company back at El Abeid. The Legion is our home now, sir, Legio patria nostra.'

'Good lad' said Captain Foster.

'So sir, why are we going to Mexico?' asked Mick.

Foster asked Roumis to go and fetch another bottle of wine as the sun began to sink below the Atlantic horizon, Roumis returned with it and gave it to Foster, who had a huge gulp, then passed the bottle to Mick to pass around the men.

'Well boys, that's a deep, deep question. I could just tell you that we're being sent to Mexico to save the asses of our colleagues in the Imperial Army, but that's not the whole story, are you sure you want to know?'

The men's silence indicated to Foster that they wanted to know more, so, against his orders, he decided to tell them.

Captain Foster then gave his men quite the impromptu history lesson.

Chapter Twenty -Seven –

Poor Old Mexico

Mexico had struggled as a state since winning its independence from Spain in 1821. Almost from day one, the new country had been split between those who favoured a liberal democracy modeled on the libertarian political model of the United States, and those who favoured a more conservative state, with a strong centralised government and strong influence from the church and former Spanish nobility, who still held much of what little wealth Mexico still had. These divisions had, over the last forty years, not only weakened Mexico's development as a state, but also made the Catholic state vulnerable to its Protestant neighbour to the north, The United States.

The United States, for its part, saw its Catholic neighbour not only as a 'soft-touch' militarily, but also as a potential threat to the great American democratic experiment. British Canada to its north and Catholic Mexico to its south might one day unite and extinguish the flames of Manifest Destiny; at least, that's what some Americans feared. Britain was the world's great superpower, so America decided to capitalise on the divisions of its weaker, Catholic neighbour to the south, and thus grab more land and secure America from the European threat, a threat which in reality, had never really existed.

First, in Texas in 1836, American settlers and a few disgruntled Tejanos – Mexican Texans – rose up and declared independence from Mexico, egged on by some in Washington but not publicly backed by the US Government. At the time, Mexico had a dictator, Antonio Lopez de Santa Anna, and at first he crushed two Texan rebel forces at The Alamo and at Goliad, but made the mistake of massacring surrendering Texans at both engagements. He had intended , like Cromwell in Ireland centuries earlier, that this brutality would deter further resistance – in fact, it galvanised the people of Texas, who soon afterwards defeated Santa Anna   and

Mexico's army at San Jacinto Bridge. Texas became an independent republic for nine years, but joined the USA in 1845.

In 1838-39, it was France's turn to invade Mexico, in what became known as the 'Pastry War'.

Mexico had run up huge debts to France, so the French sent an expedition to Mexico. Few soldiers died on either side, but Mexico was ultimately humiliated, having to pay 600,000 pesos to the French, virtually bankrupting the country. The French wanted more, but Britain managed to persuade them to withdraw, with a mix of diplomacy and military threats.

Then in 1846, The USA invaded Mexico itself, using the pretext of unpaid debts and an incident on the disputed border with Texas that saw a few American soldiers killed. Mexico had no armoury of its own for making weapons, and its troops were armed with second-hand Napoleonic-era weapons and tactics imported from Europe, while America's army was far superior both in equipment and tactics.

Despite this, Mexico fought bravely to the last, and the war did not end until US soldiers stormed into Mexico City in late 1847, with a peace treaty being signed in early 1848. The peace treaty made Mexico recognise the US annexation of Texas, and also gave the Americans California, with its gold fields, and also most of New Mexico, Arizona, Utah, Nevada and Colorado. Within 30 years of winning independence from Spain, Mexico had lost 55% of its sovereign territory to its aggressive northern neighbour.

Mexico seldom had the same government for more than a year, mostly because of its near constant state of poverty and the perpetual constitutional disputes between the liberals and the conservatives.

Things finally came to a head between 1857 and 1860, when the Liberal side won the inevitable civil conflict, the 'War of Reform', and their leader, Benito Juarez, became Mexico's elected President.

Most conservative leaders fled to Europe in the wake of their defeat, to seek foreign aid.

The civil war had depleted Mexico's treasury even further, and Juarez was forced to suspend payments of foreign debts in 1861, his main creditors being Britain, France and Spain.

The three European powers agreed to send a naval force to Mexico to enforce the repayments. Most of the Mexican debt was owed to Britain and Spain – France only became a creditor after its Emperor, Napoleon III, bought a substantial amount of Swiss bonds, which turned out to be linked to Mexico's debt. A lucky escape for the Swiss bank – a humiliation for Napoleon III – but also an opportunity for a harebrained scheme on the part of France's Emperor, who was all too happy to promise assistance to the exiled Mexican conservatives, under certain harebrained conditions.

In late 1861, the combined fleets arrived at Vera Cruz and landed troops, seizing the customs house there, and sending a column and representatives inland to negotiate with Juarez's government.

Spain sent 6000 troops and Britain sent barely a thousand soldiers between them with the expedition, while France initially landed 2000 marines and 800 Zouaves. Britain and Spain were horrified when they found out that Napoleon III had also later sent 5000 additional men, commanded by Charles Ferdinand Latrille, Comte de Lorencez, as an advance guard of what would eventually be a force of over 30,000. France had a very different agenda from that of its allies and intended not only to collect the debts, but to install its own puppet government in Mexico, replacing the legitimately elected Juarez regime with a monarchy – the very institution that Mexico had fought to rid itself of some 40 years earlier when Mexico had won independence from Spain.

Britain and Spain wanted nothing to do with this enterprise, or with imposing regime change in Mexico and, realising that blood could not be gotten from a stone, and seething at being lied to by The French, they withdrew their ships and men on April 11th, 1862, and wrote off the debt. The French Empire then declared war on the Mexican Republic.

France's intervention was supported by the conservatives who had fought against Juarez in the civil war, and by much of the clergy, and even by some Mexican Indians. It was also supported by Mexico's exiled nobility, who saw a chance to give Mexico a monarchy, while the neighbouring United States was preoccupied with its own civil war. Mexico's army, such as it was, was split, with about one quarter of it siding with the French and their allied

Mexican conservatives or Afrancesados, and the rest siding with Juarez's legitimate, Liberal, Republican cause.

Napoleon III's choice for Mexico's new puppet monarch was the Austrian Duke Maximilian of Hapsburg, younger brother of Austria's Emperor. As it turned out, Maximilian was to be Emperor, not King of Mexico. Napoleon III envisaged a pro-French empire in Central America, allowing France access to South America's lucrative silver-trade and other Latin-American markets. For his part, Maximilian was, in essence, a good, pious man, whose liberal policies actually differed very little from those of Juarez, and Maximilian also firmly believed that the church must be upheld, and that he had a duty as emperor to improve the lives of his people and the infrastructure of his new empire. Mexico was to be modernised, dragged into the industrial age, and made into a Franco-Mexican version of the United States, but with the added stability of having an Emperor as well as a token legislature. Napoleon III also promised Maximilian 10,000 European troops as a permanent standing army to back up his regime. Napoleon III had it all figured out.

There was one problem with his big plan, though.

No-one had asked the people of Mexico what they wanted.

A huge explosion of Juarez's gunpowder store and arsenal at Chalchicomula on 6th March 1862 had robbed Juarez's army of much of its gunpowder, rifles, ammunition, stores, horses and most tragically, nearly 2000 of its best soldiers, including many of Juarez's best officers, all of whom were engulfed in a gigantic fireball, which also killed hundreds of Mexican civilians. Some said it was an accident, others suspected sabotage by Afrancesados agents. Whatever the cause, Juarez and Mexico remained defiant, despite this tragedy.

The ordinary Mexican people and their army, under General Ignacio Zaragoza, responded by giving the over-confident French Regular Army and their Afrancesados allies a bloody nose at the Battle of Puebla on May 5th 1862. Zaragoza died of disease shortly after the great victory of 'Cinco de Mayo' and was replaced at Puebla by General Ortega. The defeat at Puebla stunned the French, who summoned more troops, including some elements of their

Foreign Legion, to Mexico to bolster their numbers. The Comte de Lorencez was soon relieved of command and sent home.

France, Napoleon III and Maximilian planned to stay.

Most of Mexico planned to kick them out.

Chapter Twenty-Eight –

Jimmy And Le Boudin

Jesus, that voyage.

It was pleasant enough but oh so boring.

The only entertainments that we had were betting on rats or weevils racing, or listening to Captain Foster's interesting tales about America, about Magenta, and his interpretations of why we were being sent to Mexico, of all places.

Mick and I soon realised that once again, we were fighting on the 'wrong' side. However, ours was not to reason why, ours was but to do or die, and we were fighting for our country, that is, The Legion, so we forgot about our personal feelings regarding the campaign. Mick seemed more troubled than me by this dilemma, but in the end we, and the men, all agreed that our duty was to The Legion, and to each other.

As we neared Vera Cruz, we noticed that our ships were being trailed by enormous sharks, huge things that looked like sea monsters to us. A few of the lads grabbed their rifles and tried to take pot-shots at them for sport, but the officers soon put a stop to that particular waste of ammunition.

As we sailed into Vera Cruz after about seven weeks at sea, we were overpowered, not by awe, but by disgust.

The seaward approach to Vera Cruz was littered with wrecks of ships, old and new, that had ran aground over the centuries on sand banks and had never been cleared away. The city itself also stank, almost like an open sewer, and instead of paved streets, it had mostly earthen footpaths, many of which were covered in grass, and manure. Vera Cruz was not an impressive city nor a welcoming port. It was a walled city, but the walls were in a poor state of repair, and had apparently been so since the Americans had wrecked the place in 1847. The city's one redeeming feature was its people. Much of the city's populace had fled to the areas of Mexico controlled by the legitimate Mexican President, Juarez, leaving many of the city's buildings vacant. However, we liked the Mexican people. They were mostly ordinary people like us, farmers, builders, servants, tradesmen and shopkeepers. We could tell that most of them didn't actually want us there, but they knew that we had been ordered to Mexico, and as long as we were civil to them they were civil to us. We behaved, and so did they.

We had to. We remembered what a hostile populace had done to our Emperor's uncle's Grand Armee in Spain between 1809 and 1813.

The French Regular Army units who landed were quickly moved inland, as the lands directly behind Vera Cruz were disease breeding swamps, but initially, we in The Legion remained at Vera Cruz, as we had been assigned the duty of escorting the supply trains up to the main force, which was about to have another crack at the Mexicans in Puebla. We trudged back and forth from Vera Cruz, having the dirty job of escorting the supplies across the most putrid of terrain, losing men to disease every day.

We saw precious little of the enemy. We knew there was some enemy cavalry about, but they rarely bothered us, and never attacked us with any degree of ferocity. In fact, in those first few weeks, the fiercest combat that we had was when our company had a brawl with a company of Mexican soldiers who were on our side! They were called the Veracruzano Fusileros or something like that, they were Vera Cruz's official garrison, they wore red uniforms, and they were horrible to Roumis one evening when we got back from our tedious trudging. They had never seen an Arab before, and one of them made a disgusting remark, a remark that resulted in 3rd company giving the 'Fusileros' a right good beating that night after a few bottles of pinard. After that, our Mexican allies seemed a bit scared of us, but they never once hassled Roumis or any other Legionnaire again. Vera Cruz wasn't the best posting for us, its one consolation being that we often got fresh meat and vegetables, as we were based so close to a port and market. While the army inland was eating hardtack biscuits and soup, we were eating fresh vegetables, tortillas, fish, and our favourite – fresh pork, courtesy of the HQ Company's charcutier.

Roumis wouldn't eat the pork at all, so Mick and I often got his share to eat. The whole company loved one particular style of pork that the charcutier made, it was called Boudin, that sort of black pudding sausage we'd had at Sidi. It was quite delicious, and before devoured, it often looked a bit like the rolled up blankets that we put on top of our packs on the march. We loved this Boudin. We had two young Belgian lads in our 3rd company, no older than 17, I think, and they never got any Boudin because they always missed it being served, due to the fact that they were orderlies at HQ during the day. When they got back to our little camp at night, we often teased them, singing a song that we had made up about this 'Boudin' and about how Belgians didn't get any because they were away 'shirking' at HQ all day.

We sang it to the tune of one of the old bugle calls, and sometimes we changed the words, depending on our mood, or how much pinard we had drank. The Belgian lads took it all in good humour. It relieved the monotony, and anything that did that was welcome.

Roumis wasn't just abstaining from eating pork. A double tragedy struck our company one Sunday.

We woke in the morning ready to brew coffee, but Roumis never emerged from his tent, despite the urges of his copains. I went over to his tent and saw him. He was sitting upright, wearing only his boots and his Kepi, rocking back and forth, gibbering to himself in Arabic. I called Dicken over to try and speak to him, but Roumis' eyes were glazed over, and he just looked right through Dicken too. We fetched the surgeon, and the surgeon's face fell within seconds of observing Roumis' behaviour.

'Le Cafard' said the surgeon. 'He hasn't been eating either, look at his sunken eyes and his stomach'.

We were heartbroken. We had always assumed that Roumis was the only one who would never get le Cafard, but here in Mexico, everything was different. The surgeon asked me to speak with him outside the tent. By now Mick had come over, and the surgeon asked him to help us to carry Roumis to our makeshift hospital in Vera Cruz, and we agreed. Then we heard a click, and then a BANG, and a thud.

We looked inside the tent and immediately puked our guts up.

Roumis had blown his own brains out with a revolver. Our little Arab comrade was dead! His blood and brains were splattered all over the tent.

This troubled us deeply, so much so that the surgeon got two Legionnaires from another company to clean up the mess. Dicken didn't say a word, in fact, he was never the same again. He was a quiet type at the best of times, but after that, he was silence personified. Mick and I were also distraught, and then, things got even worse.

I told the surgeon that I would go and inform Captain Foster of Roumis' death, and the surgeon just stared at the ground. Then he lifted his head and spoke.

'My friends, it is my sad duty to inform you that Captain Foster died in the middle of the night. He was overcome with a terrible fever and died within a few hours, though we think he had been ill for some days but had concealed his illness. It was El Vomito.'

We had only just gotten to know him.

We were stunned. Our trusted Captain, and our wee Arab friend, both dead! We had loved Roumis like a brother, and we would have followed Captain Foster into the very gates of Hell if he'd asked us to. Now both were gone, and killed not by bullet or blade, but by this hot, accursed, disease ridden patch of land and its merciless climate.

We had little time to mourn. We buried Roumis and the Captain with simple ceremony, and almost as soon as we had finished our prayers, we received orders telling us that our company, and indeed the whole Legion brigade, was to be sent further inland, to a place called Chiquihuite, where our commander, Colonel Jeanningros, had been told to relocate his HQ to. So we got on with it. It was our job. C'est la Legion.

Chapter Twenty-Nine – Mick's Mexico

I searched my soul a lot during that voyage to Mexico. I thought of the millions of my countrymen who had traversed that same ocean in search of a better life. I thought long and hard about whether or not we were fighting a just war, and whether or not I was a hypocrite, being Irish, yet being part of an army that did to other countries and peoples what the British had did to mine. In the end though, I decided to put my doubts to the back of my mind. I was a Legionnaire now. The Legion was my country, and my copains were my brothers. Besides, I learned to look at my situation another way – I was an Irish soldier in French service, kind of like Patrick Sarsfield, but without the horse or the Marshal's baton. In essence, I was following a path that thousands of Irishmen before me had trodden. So that was that. C'est la Legion, and all that.

I was gutted when Foster and Roumis died, they were our friends, not just our comrades in arms.

I started to fear that Foster would be replaced with a staff officer, a fear shared by most of the company. Foster had been a fighting captain, a hero, Christ knows who we might have got next.

Our duties left us little time to mourn, we were soon ordered to leave Vera Cruz for Chiquihuite, our new base further inland. I think that the day Roumis died, something inside Dicken died, for he was never the same again. He became even more silent and sullen, yet still our friend, our copain.

I wasn't sad to see the back of Vera Cruz at all, the place stank, and we didn't get on well with the Mexican regiment stationed there at all. With allies like them, who needs enemies? One thing did kind of worry us – we were told that hardly any French horses had survived the voyage across the Atlantic, they had all died of disease en route, or had broken legs at sea and had to be destroyed. All in all, our whole French army in Mexico had no more than 200 cavalrymen – we would have to rely on our 'allies' to provide extra cavalry support, that wasn't good news at all, but we just got on with things. For a few weeks we trudged up and down the Vera Cruz road escorting wagons back and forth, as we had did in our first week in

Mexico, only now we were losing fellas every day to sickness, disease and le Cafard.

It really didn't look like we were going to see much action either, no, our friends in the Regular Army were going to get all the glory on this campaign, or so we thought...

Chapter Thirty- Showdown

On Thursday the 30th of April, 1863, unbeknownst to the French High Command or their Mexican Afrancesados allies, a strong force of Juarez's Mexican infantry and cavalry, over two brigades in total, and their irregular allies, was sent to capture a well-laden, valuable but scantily guarded French supply convoy, which was known to be somewhere between Vera Cruz and Cordoba. The Mexicans planned to seize the convoy's supplies, slaughter its escorting force of Legionnaires, and possibly end the war in one fell swoop. Before the 30th of April 1863, The Republican/Juarez-led army of Mexico and the soldiers of the French Foreign Legion had never faced each other in direct combat. If one could locate the other, they finally would face each other. An unstoppable force was about to run into a near immovable object. This is how history was made.

Chapter Thirty – One - Jimmy's Battle

Though our counterparts and comrades in France's Imperial Army and their Afrancesados allies had been checked by the Mexicans the previous May at The Battle of Puebla, by the spring of 1863 the French Army under General Forey had advanced inland once more, in greater strength, leaving behind the sweltering heat of the fetid coastal-plane and climbing slowly but steadily into the cooler, healthier uplands of Mexico's central plateau. When the French Army reached Puebla again, the Mexicans turned to once more make a stand, but this time were compelled to give up the field without a serious fight, instead packing some of their army into outlying forts and into Puebla itself, while the rest of the army retreated still further inland. Forey's army was compelled to lay siege to Puebla. This meant that Forey's lines of communication and supply back to Vera Cruz now stretched for just over 150 miles. Almost as soon as France's army closed the circle around Puebla, the supply lines began to come under sporadic attack by bands of Mexican lancers and irregulars, known as Guerrilleros. They only attacked the smaller supply columns, avoiding full-scale engagements, preferring instead to ride into rifle range, fire a few ragged volleys from their carbines, and then melt away back into the countryside. Since Forey had hardly any cavalry of his own with which to take them on, most of France's cavalry horses having not survived the Trans-Atlantic voyage, the only thing that could be done to counter these raids was to set up a series of small outposts along the supply route from the coast to Puebla. These little fortified outposts were roughly twenty miles apart. That was where The Legion, we, came in. General Forey knew that the vile, disease infested land between Vera Cruz and what was essentially the halfway point between the coast and Puebla, Cordoba, where we had an outpost, was no country for European soldiers to serve in, so The Legion was given the task of defending and protecting the supply route, as being Legionnaires, it didn't matter as much to Forey, or to the rest of the army, if it was The Legion who suffered the worst of all the ghastly tropical diseases and malarial insects that infested the route. We were only

The Legion, expendable, and once again, we had been given the dirtiest of jobs to do, another thankless, dangerous task with, it seemed, little chance of action.

However, we expected nothing more than this, and we suspected that our being allocated this role was in part down to the fact that The Legion's own High Command had went over the Regular Army's head to directly petition the French Emperor to allow us to be part of the Mexican campaign. And so it was that we found ourselves tramping around in the hot, damned dirty dust and fetid swamps once more, but that was our job, and as we consoled ourselves – C'est la Legion!

After only a few weeks of manning the little outposts and escorting the convoys, the vile diseases which plagued the area had severely thinned our ranks. Men died of Typhus, Malaria, Cholera, Yellow Fever and a mysterious sickness that made men die by vomiting black mucus. Not only that, Le Cafard had proved a hardy 'species' of disease, and had followed The Legion to Mexico, where it thrived.

Men became gibbering wrecks and had to be hospitalised. Some shot themselves or opened their guts with their own bayonets to escape Le Cafard, others, delirious, became almost useless and had to be left in the fortified outposts until they had recovered, unable to go out on patrol.

By mid-April, Mexico's heat and inhospitable climate had thinned our ranks to such a level that not a single Legion company was at full strength, and officers weren't any safer from the climate than Legionnaires were. Our own 3rd company was led by our senior NCO, Sergeant-Major Tonel -Lieutenant Brandt, Captain Foster and a number of officers having died of the mysterious vomiting sickness. I felt sad about the loss of our officers, they'd come all this way to Mexico, having survived the battles in Algeria, only, like so many ordinary soldiers, to die in their own puke, blood and shit in this God-forsaken land. Just as worrying was the shortage of officers. Most of us would rather serve under a promoted NCO than under some staff officer who didn't know his arse from his elbow, and who didn't know us.

But again, C'est La Legion.

The Legion was based at Chiquihuite, where Colonel Jeanningros had established our headquarters, and it was from there that we sent patrols and convoy escorts to cover the badlands between Vera Cruz and Cordoba. On the 27th of April, hearing that a large, 64 wagon convoy from Vera Cruz was heading our way, Colonel Jeanningros sent back two companies of our brother Legionnaires to reinforce this convoy's escort. I later found out that the convoy, which had been crawling at a snail's pace towards us for almost two weeks, was carrying not just supplies, but ammunition and heavy artillery for Forey's army at Puebla, which was gradually reducing the Mexican General Ortega's defensive perimeter. Now Forey needed heavy guns with which to utterly smash Puebla's defences and so open the road to Mexico City. General Forey had expressly ordered that we in The Legion were to play no part either in the storming of Puebla or in the march on Mexico City. The supply convoy wasn't just carrying artillery, supplies and munitions though, it was also carrying the army's pay chests – over three million gold francs, which would be used to pay the army and also to pay for much of its irregular Mexican support from the Mexican Afrancesados.

We were boiling coffee on the evening of the 29th when one of our own Indian scouts rode into camp, hurriedly dismounted and then headed straight for the colonel's tent. He emerged from the tent after about ten minutes and rode off once more. Sergeant-Major Tonel soon came over to tell us to get our kit and weapons together – the scout had brought news that a huge Mexican force, including many of the 'regulars' that we had thus far been unable to locate, was planning to attack the convoy and seize its precious cargo of gold and munitions. The only thing our Colonel didn't know was the time and location that the Mexican attack was planned for.

Our once proud 3rd company of the 1st Battalion had numbered 120 men when we arrived in Mexico, now, as we mustered in the growing darkness in the eerie light of our camp fires, only 62 of us remained, including our temporary leader, Sergeant-Major Tonel.

As we stood in a column of twos, three figures approached us and then ordered us to face-left, so that we were facing them. One of our worst fears was realised as we got a better look at the three men.

They were our new officers, and they were staff officers from the HQ detachment! The senior of the three introduced himself as Captain Danjou, the battalion adjutant and quartermaster. We all recognised him as he only had one good arm. Where his left-forearm had once been, he wore a peculiar, almost absurd looking wooden hand -we were to be led not only by a staff officer, but by one who was an amputee!

The other two officers, both Second-Lieutenants, were also staff officers from the HQ detachment, Maudet, and Vilain, the latter being the regimental pay-master. None of us in the ranks spoke, but I could tell that we were all thinking the same thing – we were to be led by administrators, not fighting officers. Then I remembered Foster telling me about Captain Danjou during the voyage from Oran to Vera Cruz. Danjou may have been performing staff duties, but he was a 'real' officer. He had lost his hand in 1853 in Algeria when his rifle had misfired and its breech exploded, but he had carried on with his career despite his disability, and more than proved himself to still be of fighting quality, having survived both The Crimean Expedition of 1854-56, and the slaughterhouse that was the Battle of Magenta in 1859. Remembering that, my apprehension faded away a little, and I was sure that most of my copains had also heard about the tall, thin officer called Captain Danjou, and his wooden hand. As for the other two officers, we didn't have a clue, but we would, if need be, follow them and the one-handed Captain into the very gates of Hell if we were ordered to do so – C'est la Legion!

Captain Danjou didn't speak to us for very long before we marched out, but one simple sentence that passed his lips stayed in all of our heads. 'We march to find and join the convoy and to re-enforce its escort, the convoy must get through, no matter what the cost. The convoy is important, our lives are not.'

Just before we marched out of Chiquihuite at around midnight, Sergeant-Major Tonel quietly informed us all that intelligence indicated that the supply convoy was indeed to be attacked, but that we shouldn't worry too much about the Guerrilleros – they were more of a nuisance than a serious military threat, and the Indian scout had probably greatly exaggerated the threat of being attacked by Mexico's actual army.

We were to march back down the Vera-Cruz road towards the small hamlet of Palo Verde, over twenty miles away. If we encountered the convoy en route, we had orders to join its escort, though no-one actually knew just where the convoy was. If we encountered neither the convoy nor the enemy before reaching Palo Verde, we were simply to return to Chiquihuite and finally get some well earned sleep.

Our orders seemed simple enough, however, one contingency had not been planned for – not encountering the convoy on the way to Palo Verde but being attacked on the march back.

And so, we set out, each of us carrying full kit, A Scotsman, an Irishman, an Englishman, Frenchmen, Poles, Germans, Italians and even two seventeen-year old Belgians, with 60 rounds per man and each of us carrying one canteen of water. A further 40 rounds per man, extra water and all of our rations were packed onto a few mules, to slightly ease our burden. 65 men, six mules, and on this march, we were not permitted to sing. Among our other NCOs were corporals Maine and Berg, both ferocious fighters, veterans of a dozen battles, who like Tonel, we had great respect for. We expected no trouble, but we were ever ready for it.

At first the march was like any other, tedious, but then we came to Paso Del Macho (Place of the Mules) at about 2am. One of our Grenadier companies was stationed there, so we stopped to drink and have a brief rest. The Grenadiers' own Captain appeared horrified by our lack of numbers and offered Captain Danjou one of his own platoons as reinforcements. Danjou politely refused the offer, no doubt as he was eager to cover as much ground as possible in the cool of the night, rather than wait thirty or forty minutes for the Grenadier platoon to be woken and assembled so that it could join us.

We resumed the march, making good time, and shortly before 7am we reached an abandoned village, mostly consisting of a few tiny mud-brick dwellings, one slightly larger mud-brick dwelling, and a large, abandoned two-storey Hacienda, which was surrounded by a partially broken wall some nine or ten feet high.

We passed through the deserted village without incident. That village's name was Camerone.

After reaching Palo Verde, our destination, Captain Danjou ordered us to rest briefly, so we stopped on a low rise in the ground to brew some coffee, and we posted sentries and piled our rifles. We were all looking forward to the coffee, which was much improved from the stuff we drank in Algeria as it was locally produced. We hadn't seen so much as a Coyote on the march, nor was there any sign of the convoy, and we were now bathed in the early morning sun.

We never got to drink any coffee though.

As soon as our kettles began to boil, our sentries came sprinting towards us, reporting seeing a huge dust cloud to our west, a dust cloud that could only indicate one thing – a large body of enemy cavalry.

Our Captain now had a number of decisions to make, and he had to make them quickly.

He could relinquish our one horse, his own, and send one of the second-lieutenants on it to Soledad, where the convoy probably was, to warn the convoy about the enemy cavalry. However, in all probability, the convoy was well aware that it was in danger from the Mexicans, and was maybe even waiting at Soledad for its reinforcements, i.e., us, so Danjou sent no courier. We therefore had three realistic options. We could make a dash for Soledad, assuming that's where the convoy was, but that was far too risky and could easily have seen us hacked to pieces in the open by the Mexican cavalry.

Our second option was to remain at Palo Verde and defend ourselves, utilising what scant cover there was, but that too could have resulted in us being quickly over-run to no real purpose, and that would be of no benefit to the convoy.

The third and final option, which Captain Danjou ultimately decided on, was to move westward, towards the advancing Mexican cavalry but using the tall scrub beside the road as partial cover, back to that village, where we could take up a proper defensive position, or perhaps make for a nearby Indian village where we might expect to find some help.

Mick and I doused the camp fires as the rest of the lads loaded our supplies back onto our mules, and we began marching westward, back to that place called Camerone. We put out a small advance guard and flankers, while the main body of us, including Mick, myself and Dicken, marched in two thin columns, bayonets fixed and glinting in the sun, so that we could quickly form a defensive square if, and when, the Mexican cavalry discovered us.

We made it to the outskirts of Camerone once more, and then, from nowhere, a single shot rang out and one of our advance guard fell to the ground, severely wounded. No further shots came though, so we marched on, until we had left Camerone about a mile behind us. Our hopes of reaching safety were soon dashed though, as across our front, a huge mass of Mexican cavalry finally cantered into full view.

We would not be making for the Indian village now; they were right across our path. Even without field-glasses I could see that the enemy cavalry wasn't just made up of Guerrilleros – there were lancers, and other cavalrymen too, and to my horror, I saw that they were wearing old Napoleonic era style uniforms – they were regulars!

As soon as they spotted us, they charged. I looked at Mick, and he winked at me as he loaded his rifle, which in turn made me load my own. Captain Danjou dismounted and ordered us to form square, which we did, though it was a tiny square with just 64 fit men in it, one wounded man sheltering in the hollow centre. The Captain turned his own horse loose, and as he did so, I saw the determination in his face – one way or another, we were going to make history today.

Being in the square as the Mexicans came on was a mixed blessing. We knew that their horses would not charge onto our little hedge of bayonets, but on the other hand, we couldn't exactly remain in the square all day, as if the Mexicans were savvy they would just whittle away the square's strength with their firearms before rushing in to finish off the survivors. But the Mexicans were not savvy at first, and walked their horses to within 50 yards of our square before charging us from two sides with swords and lances. No doubt they expected us to buckle and run under their attack, many regular troops would have did so, but we were not 'regular' troops, we were Legionnaires, and this kind of thing was all in a day's work for the veterans of Algeria. When the Mexicans got to within 30 paces of our square, Captain Danjou ordered us to fire two volleys, then to fire independently.

The front ranks of the Mexican cavalry were flattened by the precision fire from our rifled muskets – not one horseman got near our square, and we cheered loudly as they retreated, but though their courage and pride had been tested, they kept their nerve and began to circle our tiny square, just out of range of our long-barreled rifles. Captain Danjou knew what was coming next.

He knew that we couldn't stay where we were, and that our only option now was to fight our way back to Camerone to take up a stronger position – easier said than done. Our square struggled to keep its tight formation as we moved through the scrub, some of us walking backwards, and the gaps that inevitably opened up allowed the Mexican cavalry to ride in, and we started to lose men. I saw one Mexican Lancer charge towards Mick, screaming 'bastardo' as he bore down on him. Mick was in the middle of reloading and roared back at him 'Soy Irlandes, you bastardo' as he replaced his ramrod and reached for a percussion cap. He dropped the percussion cap, so I leveled my own rifle at the Lancer and squeezed my trigger, but to my dismay, I had forgotten to put a cap on my rifle's nipple, and nothing happened. I needn't have worried. Mick simply turned his rifle about and smacked the Mexican's horse on the nose twice, making it go berserk and throw its rider. Mick's bayonet was stuck in the Lancer's heart as soon as he hit the ground, then Mick picked up the man's lance and hurled it like a javelin at another Mexican horseman who had been about to slash me. He too fell from his mount, blood pouring from his mouth, the thrown lance through his chest. Mick unslung his rifle again and the both of us continued our independent fire, as did the rest of our little company, as we edged closer to the village, Camerone, where we could make a proper stand. Despite almost being over-run, our square held. I'll never forget seeing Captain Danjou's own unique way of dealing with Mexican cavalry. He simply beheaded the horse with his sabre, then slashed the rider to death as he was thrown forwards off the dead horse's back.

The retreat wasn't a complete success. We lost about a dozen men, killed, wounded or missing, but worst of all, in the confusion, our normally docile Mules had bolted in terror, taking with them our rations, our much-needed reserve ammunition and even worse, our precious water.

There was little time to dwell on that loss. We were surrounded by over 800 Mexican horsemen.

They should really have just ridden us down en masse, but the ferocity of our resistance and the casualties that they suffered seemed to temporarily un-nerve them, and miraculously, we made it back to Camerone, though we were not more than 50 strong by then, and to our horror, we discovered that the upper floor of the building that Danjou had selected for our defensive position, The Hacienda Del Trinidad, was in fact occupied by some enemy snipers. The Hacienda offered us great protection, and even with one of its three gates missing and numerous big holes in the walls, we were now safe from cavalry charges.

The Mexicans in the upper part of the building could only fire at certain parts of the courtyard, because of the size of the wall that protected them up there, so Captain Danjou assigned the two seventeen year-old Belgians to keep their heads down, which they did, as the rest of us began to try to shore up the Hacienda's crumbling walls and the non-existent gate as best we could. Mick said 'just like old times' to me as we stuffed boulders into some of the breaches in the walls, referring to our days in Edinburgh as builders. That seemed like an eternity ago, but we both laughed.

Captain Danjou and the two second lieutenants made sure that we had shored up the defences, and had us make loopholes in the walls wherever we could. We had the bottom floor of the Hacienda well loopholed, we had that nine or ten foot wall around the courtyard, which was barely 60 metres square, also well-loopholed, and there was a stable in the corner that we could shelter in, or on top of.

Schwarz, the big man from Alsace, perched on that, lying flat. Curiously, we had no access to the upper floor of the Hacienda, but it was clear that the Mexicans had no direct access to us from there either. Whatever happened next, we had done our best to prepare our defences, the next move would be the Mexicans'.

Schwarz shouted from the stable roof, and Dicken, without any prompting, shouted to Mick and I in translation. The Mexicans were dismounting and removing their spurs, a sure sign that they were preparing to storm our little fortress. They had also been joined by a battalion of Mexican regular infantry. I was pleased to be beside my friend Mick, and I apologised to him for dragging him into this sorry mess. He replied with a grin 'Jimmy lad, if I wasn't here, who else would watch your back? I'm here because I want to be.'

At about 9.30am, following a brief exchange of fire, a Mexican officer approached under a white flag, and Captain Danjou went out to meet him. The Mexican officer demanded our immediate surrender.

Captain Danjou replied that he had plenty of ammunition and had no intention of surrendering.

The Mexican officer looked surprised, then tried to appeal to Captain Danjou's compassionate side by urging him not to waste his men's lives so needlessly, when they were so hopelessly outnumbered and surrounded – why not give his men a say, a chance to save their lives? Captain Danjou smirked and told the Mexican officer that he would ask us, and that he would have his answer within five minutes – a white flag if we chose to surrender, a surprise if we did not. The Mexican officer agreed and both officers returned to their men.

Captain Danjou conversed with Vilain and Maudet briefly upon his return, I saw both of the 2nd lieutenants shake their heads disdainfully, scornfully, before I turned back to my loophole and waited for the inevitable Mexican attack. We all waited, rifles loaded and cocked. Then Mick spoke to me.

'Jimmy, I'm no expert but these here Mexicans are packing a lot more firepower than us. They've all got repeaters. They can fire seven shots to every two that we fire, and there's a lot more of them too.'

'Well?' I said.

'Good Irishman's odds' he said.

'Good Scotsman's odds too' said I. We both laughed.

Just then I felt something on my shoulder, I turned my head and saw that it was Captain Danjou's wooden hand. He waved Dicken over to Mick and I, as it was Dicken who spoke the best French, and then he gave us all a single swig of Pinard from his personal liter. The wine tasted ghastly in the heat, but we drank it all the same, thinking that it would be our last sip of wine. The Captain spoke briefly and calmly, but with a fire in his eyes that we had never noticed before, as if he was telling an after dinner anecdote. Dicken quickly translated Danjou's words.

'My comrades, my children, the force that is attacking us is the force that the Mexicans sent to attack the supply convoy. Every minute, every second that we hold them here buys time for the convoy. The longer we delay these stupid asses here, the better for the convoy, for The Legion and for France – do you swear to fight to the death alongside me, to the bitter end? It will be an honour to die among you, mes enfants.'

His words chilled us, but they also filled our hearts with pride.

The three of us answered in unison – 'oui mon capitaine'.

The one-handed Captain Danjou was as brave as a Lion.

Captain Danjou smiled, then hurried around the courtyard with his wine, never trying to dodge bullets, exacting the same oath from every man, even from our drummer, who had just staggered in with no less than seven lance wounds. Danjou then sprinted over to Sergeant Major Tonel, who in turn roared out to us.

'Listen up men, are you going to surrender?'

'NON' we all roared in unison.

'Very well men, now, remember that song you've all been singing in camp and on the march recently, the one about the charcutier and the sausage and the Belgians, sing it, sing it loud, altogether, sing!'

Despite our dry mouths, we sang as loudly as we could, that special song, the words of which we hadn't even finished writing.

'Tiens, voilà du boudin, voilà du boudin, voilà du boudin
Pour les Alsaciens, les Suisses et les Lorrains,
pour les Belges y en a plus,
pour les Belges y en a plus,
ce sont des tireurs au cul

pour les Belges y en a plus,
pour les Belges y en a plus,
ce sont des tireurs au cul
Tiens, voilà du boudin, voilà du boudin, voilà du boudin
Pour les Alsaciens, les Suisses et les Lorrains!'

The song was the 'no surrender' signal that Captain Danjou had promised the Mexicans, and the message got through loud and clear, for as soon as we had stopped singing, we heard an enraged cry of 'fuego', and in an instant , hundreds upon hundreds of bullets rained into our little fortress. To us it sounded like hailstones pattering against the outer wall relentlessly, and it turned out that Mick had been right about the Mexicans having Sharps or Spencer repeating rifles. A torrent of fire was poured into our position, wounding some of us, killing some of us, each man a copain loved and respected.

Then it was our turn. We leveled our rifled-muskets at the dismounted Mexican cavalry and the regular infantry, and each shot well aimed was a Mexican killed, or completely incapacitated. We took a heavy toll of them, and them of us, but we could afford far fewer losses than those who surrounded us.

We loaded and fired, loaded and fired, and we could tell that the Mexicans were enraged by our stubborn, heroic resistance. Every so often they would cease firing and attempt to rush us, but they seldom got within five yards of our little Hacienda, and eventually they went back to trying to blast us out with ceaseless hail-storms from their modern fast-firing rifles.

Then, at about mid-day, tragedy struck. A bullet struck Mick in the shoulder, making him fall backwards from his loophole, though he wasn't seriously hurt. Captain Danjou rushed over to our wall to plug the gap with his heavy Lefaucheux revolver, but was shot in the chest, I think, by one of the stubborn Mexicans who were cowering in the Hacienda's upper floor. The two seventeen year-old Belgians who had been keeping those particular enemy heads down were both lying dead, so no-one had been covering the upper floor. Poor Captain Danjou died within minutes, and Vilain took over.

'For the captain' roared Vilain, and we continued loading and firing. Mick was back on his feet, but he was aiming at the upper floor of the Hacienda. I turned around for a moment just in time to see a sombrero-clad head pop up over the parapet, and then Mick fired a minie ball straight into his face, sending blood and matter splattering into the air like a small red cloud, After that, no more firing came from the upper floor.

About half an hour after Danjou had died, Schwarz, who had somehow managed to stay on the stable roof, firing constantly without being hit, called out that more troops were coming, he could see dust, and then we heard a bugle call.Hope sprang in all our hearts.

We were sure that it was our pathetically small number of cavalry from Vera Cruz, come to rescue us, just like when the French cavalry had rescued us back at El Abeid in Algeria, or maybe it was even some of the Afrancesados soldiers coming to save us. Then Schwarz called out again.

It was neither.

Schwarz gave us the bad news. The new force that had arrived was simply more Mexican reinforcements, infantry and cavalry, and even some irregulars. More soldatos than we had ammo for.

2nd Lieutenant Vilain ran round checking the men. Almost all of us had been hit. Though the walls we defended were high, there was no firing step, so to fire from atop the wall, a Legionnaire had to stand on an upturned box or barrel, and when the Mexicans got closer, the Legionnaire had to expose a great deal of himself in order to shoot down on them, making him more vulnerable to counter fire than if he was firing from one of the loopholes. We were running low on ammunition, and there was no water left. Some of the older hands from Algeria were drinking their own urine, others, Mick included, licked blood from their own wounds just to take in a pathetic amount of moisture. Inside the Hacienda was like an oven, adding one more iota of misery to the plight of those among our wounded who were too badly hurt to keep fighting. And now, by Schwarz's reckoning, we were surrounded by over 3000 Mexicans.

Now it was the Mexicans' turn to serenade us with music, though theirs was of a purely instrumental kind. They had clearly included a marching band among their numbers, and a strange, intimidating yet rousing tune began to drift across the dry, baking hot Mexican air towards us.

The tune was haunting.

Mick turned to me and said 'if they've brought a band, they must be planning to celebrate something.'

I simply nodded and listened, but then Dicken spoke, as the haunting tune still blared at us.

'Beautiful isn't it? The tune is called El Deguello. On this continent it was originally a simple Spanish cavalry march, until the Mexicans won their independence. Then General Santa Anna adopted it in the 1830's for the Mexican army when they fought in Texas, it signals no quarter – surrender or you die.

It was played at The Alamo. The Spanish once used the tune to signal death in the Bull-ring, but the tune is even older than that – The Moors played the tune when their armies occupied Spain many centuries ago, and that's where the Spaniards pinched it from. That's the tune, El Deguello.'

'How the hell do you know that?' asked Mick.

'A bloke in the 5th company back at Sidi-Bel-Abbes once gave me some history books to wipe my arse with. I read them instead.'

I told Dicken I thought the song was beautiful.

'El Deguello means the slashed throat' he replied.

Not so beautiful.

We had traded hot lead with The Mexicans, now we were exchanging songs too!

When the haunting tune finally finished, another huge but inept series of fusillades crashed into our position, four or five volleys, showering our little fortress with thousands of bullets. We replied as best we could from our loopholes and our positions atop the wall. I had Mick and Dicken on either side of me, every time we leveled our rifles at a Mexican, the man was as good as dead.

As Vilain ran around checking the men, he sternly reminded us all of our oath to fight to the death, no matter how futile the struggle became. No-one was coming to our aid, we were alone, quite alone, but we still had a job to do.

By now I too had realised what a strategic blunder that the Mexicans had made. A huge force like the one which surrounded us was clearly the force that had been charged with attacking and stealing the big supply convoy, with all its guns, munitions, supplies, and over three million francs in gold. Yet because of The Legion's stubborn resistance here at Camerone, and the casualties that the Mexicans had suffered, they had allowed themselves to be drawn into a battle where , tactically at least, they couldn't lose, but strategically, they had messed up hugely. They could simply have bottled us up using a much smaller force until thirst compelled us to surrender, but instead, they had surrounded us with two brigades, two bloody brigades, against what had been a mere 65 Legionnaires! This made no strategic sense at all.

The Hacienda itself certainly wasn't of any strategic value. Thank God the Mexicans had no cannon!

That doesn't mean that our opponents weren't good soldiers, those Mexican boys were as good as any other men that have ever fought, it was just that they were barking up the wrong tree – wasting hundreds of their own men's lives and expending thousands of rounds of ammunition just to bottle up and try to wipe out a single, depleted Legion company – and all the while, the supply convoy could well have just passed by, right under their very sombreros.

Of course, this strategic blunder, which everyone in the Hacienda now knew about, did us no good, far from it. Every assault that we repulsed and every score of soldatos that we mowed down only stiffened their resolve to finish us of. The bullets came in the thousands now, always like a deadly storm of pattering hailstones against the walls of the Hacienda, and we lost more men to each volley, and after a while, we had to abandon some of the loopholes because we were getting so short handed.

Mick turned to me and said 'Jimmy, we're good, but this is getting ridiculous now. We must be outnumbered 50 to 1'.

He was right. As usual. Something had to give.

At about 2pm, Vilain was shot dead as we repulsed a determined attempt by the Mexicans to escalade the Hacienda and give us the bayonet. We repulsed another massed charge too, and 2nd Lieutenant Maudet took over command, and the deadly repetition of firefight followed by attempted storm, continued.

Then at about 5pm,after yet another prolonged fire-fight, a second white flag appeared , with a different Mexican officer standing under it. Maudet went to talk to him, and came back to us with the same question that we had been asked earlier – did we want to surrender? Again, we all answered 'NON', though by now there were only thirteen of us, including Maudet, who were able to stand and bear arms. We gave the Mexican officer standing outside the same answer as before, loudly.

'Tiens, voilà du boudin, voilà du boudin, voilà du boudin
Pour les Alsaciens, les Suisses et les Lorrains,
pour les Belges y en a plus,
pour les Belges y en a plus,
ce sont des tireurs au cul
pour les Belges y en a plus,
pour les Belges y en a plus,
ce sont des tireurs au cul
Tiens, voilà du boudin, voilà du boudin, voilà du boudin
Pour les Alsaciens, les Suisses et les Lorrains!'

This time, after we had finished singing, the cry from the Mexican officers was 'Adelante' rather than 'Fuego', as a battalion of Mexican regulars, resplendent in their garish Napoleonic era uniforms or plain white soldato gear , again tried to storm us. I heard a ZIP and turned round to see Dicken's near lifeless corpse slump to the ground, he growled 'empty my pockets, Jimmy' at me, before he finally died, hit by five bullets at once. I bent down and picked out his last two cartridges from his pouch, but as I did I felt something else- a tiny stone, a rock, a diamond! It was the 'insurance' diamond that Roumis had given to Dicken in that Paris café just before we joined The Legion! Without thinking I stuffed it into my boot and forgot about it, and carried on shooting and bayoneting any Mexicans who tried to get over the section of wall that Dicken, Mick and I had been defending.

Our ammunition was now almost all gone and we were using the caps and cartridges from the pouches of our dead and severely wounded comrades. We were crazed with thirst, but we were

Legionnaires, we weren't going to give in, we were now fighting not just for The Legion, not just for France, but for our heroic dead amputee captain and the oath that he had extracted from us. We weren't stupid either, though, we knew the game would soon be up. In a way, that stiffened our resolve, as we were already resigned to death, so we didn't fear it. C'est la Legion!

Then the Mexicans set the Hacienda on fire.

I remember saying a kind of prayer in my head, I'm sure we all did, even the non-believers among us, after all –there's no such thing as an Atheist on the battlefield.

The thick, black, acrid smoke made our terrible thirst even worse, but still we fought on, though we had to abandon the walls and withdraw to the little stable, as there were by now only six of us left, including 2nd Lieutenant Maudet. Schwarz had finally been shot down from the stable roof. Everybody else was either dead or severely wounded. Mick and I were still alive, with just one cartridge left each.

Corporal Maine, and Legionnaires Wenzel and Constantin were the only men still on their feet with us. They too were down to their last round.

There was nothing left to do. We couldn't surrender – we had a promise to keep to Captain Danjou.

All six of us knew what we must do next. With hundreds of Mexicans in the courtyard and thousands more waiting outside, all of them aiming their weapons at us and thirsting for our blood, we did the only honourable thing that we could do – we fired a last volley, and then, we six men charged our bayonets, and with a defiant roar, we attacked the two brigades of Mexicans.

Chapter Thirty-Two – Mick's Battle

I'll never forget what happened that day, at that little place in Mexico called Camerone. The thing is, life has a habit of putting us into our most troubling situations when we are least expecting it.

On the evening of April 29th, I wasn't very happy at all when I was told that our company was to leave our little base at Chiquihuite to go back and babysit yet another supply convoy. It wasn't that I had any sense of foreboding, far from it, in fact, I was just a bit pissed off that I was going to miss out on some much needed sleep. I wasn't expecting any trouble, other than the usual, half-hearted attempts to harry us by the Mexican irregular cavalry, and they alone were never a threat, more of a pain in the arse at times.

The fact that we were being led by a one-handed staff officer didn't exactly fill me with confidence, but as they say, C'est la Legion, and one thing I've learned in life is never to judge a man by the way that he looks. He was our officer anyway, so no matter who he was, we'd have followed him into the very gates of Hell if he'd ordered us to. He was the battalion adjutant, this one handed captain in his mid 30's.

That didn't mean that me and the lads weren't a little bit wary about being led by staff officers, who we, as a rule, seldom held in high regard, but things being as they were with disease and casualties in the Legion units in Mexico, we did what The Legion always did – made the best of things and got on with the job.

By the time we left Chiquihuite that evening, our company numbered little more than 60 men, thanks to disease, wounds and le Cafard, which had not only followed us across the Atlantic from Oran, but seemed to affect men even more greatly in Mexico. Why, I don't know.

We were the only 'spare' company available to Colonel Jeanningros, so off we marched. We were to march as far as Palo Verde, and were to reinforce the supply convoy if we encountered it on the way there or on the way back. After our Captain refused the reinforcements from the Grenadiers, we never encountered anyone, friend or foe, on the march to Palo Verde, all I really remember about the march there was passing through a deserted little village just before Palo Verde, and wondering why it had been vacated by its inhabitants, and for how long, such was the tedium of the first stage of the march.

Shortly after day break or thereabouts, we posted sentries and halted to brew some morning coffee. Almost as soon as we had fallen out to rest for ten minutes, our sentries saw Mexican cavalry in the distance, and we rushed to arm ourselves, forgetting about our morning coffee. We headed straight for some long, tall grass , and in two columns we trudged as quietly as we could back towards that little village of Camerone, it was clear that the captain was leading us to the best defensive position in the area, the only question was, would we make it there without being hacked to bits en route?

As things turned out, we actually made it back to Camerone safely, marching beyond it, towards the Mexican cavalry but remaining out of sight. Captain Danjou then lead us on westward still, perhaps hoping to avoid the Mexican cavalry altogether, but we lost a man to a sniper shot on the way and were soon discovered. As we were in columns of twos, it was easy for us to quickly form a square to face the enemy cavalry, and we completely flattened their first charge, waiting until the cocky bastards had rode their horses up to within 30 paces of our tiny square before we gave them two volleys and then some independent fire. They didn't like that one bit. The mad thing is, those first two volleys we fired, I didn't actually hear them. I aimed my rifle, I fired it, downed my targets, and saw that my copains were doing the same, but for some odd reason, I remember that part of the action in slow motion, silence.

To show us that he was not going to leave our side, Captain Danjou turned his horse loose, a symbolic gesture that raised all of our spirits. However, it was clear to everyone that we couldn't just remain where we were in the square, as the Mexicans would've just did what the Arabs would have did – fired at us from a distance to whittle away our numbers, then rush us. Our mules soon bolted anyway, so we said goodbye to our reserve ammunition and our reserve water, and on Captain Danjou's command, we began the difficult job of retreating eastward, back to Camerone, but moving while still in square formation. Dicken and Jimmy were close by me.

To move while in square is difficult – to move in square while moving over broken terrain and under attack took exceptional skill. We did our best, but gaps appeared, and the second Mexican cavalry attack saw them break our square in a few places, and as well as firing, we had to defend ourselves with bayonets and rifle-butts, while the captain slashed away with his sabre. Now, this part of the battle was a bit of a 'red mist' situation for me , you know? I got angry. Like my comrades I loaded and fired, but I also got stuck into the Mexicans with my bayonet, I think I might even have thrown a downed comrade's bayonet-tipped rifle at one Mexican horseman as my rage engulfed me, or it may have been a discarded Mexican lance that I hurled at him. That part of the battle seemed to happen so fast, but our training, and our courage, saved us. We weren't going to let down ourselves, the captain, the Legion or France.

Somehow, me made it back to Camerone, and made a little 'fort' out of the big sort-of farmhouse building there. It had a ten foot wall around it, but the wall was in a right state, as were the gates to the courtyard, so we plugged them up as best we could. The upper floor of the farmhouse had a couple of enemy snipers in it, so Captain Danjou assigned those two young Belgian lads to keep their heads down as best they could, as we re-organised ourselves. We were excited but not unduly worried – we were facing cavalry, and cavalry were neither trained, equipped or provisioned to storm fortified positions – even half crumbling ones like the one our little half-company now occupied.

All in all, we lost about a dozen men during the retreat to Camerone, killed or wounded. No-one could be sure, but we thought that we must have killed or wounded at least a hundred enemy cavalry.

After we had finished shoring up the hacienda's defences as best we could, the captain positioned us at loopholes, and other points along the perimeter. I was thankful to be placed shoulder to shoulder with Jimmy and Dicken, my true friends. We were given a section of the wall to defend.

The Captain persuaded one of the men to go onto the stable roof , to give us a better idea of what we were about to face. He was quick to tell us that the Mexican cavalry were indeed huge in number, maybe 800 strong, some were irregulars, some were lancers, and some were regular cavalry. Our lookout told us that they were surrounding us and taking off their spurs, which meant that they were going to attack us directly, on foot. My heart sank a little, when our lookout, a big man from Alsace, then reported that a battalion of Mexican infantry had arrived to join the force besieging us. That wasn't so good.

Firing began.

We had already been fighting all morning, when sometime after 9am, a Mexican officer asked for and was given a parley with Captain Danjou. The captain was asked to ask us if we wanted an opportunity to save our own lives. His response, after rejoining us in our little 'Fort Camerone' was to go around us in small groups, and over a swig of wine from his own personal bottle, we swore a sacred oath to him that we would fight to the death, to the last man, to the last cartridge, no matter what occurred. I must say, this was one communion that had my heart bursting with pride, especially when the captain explained just why we had to do this. As the captain busied himself extracting the same oath from our comrades, Sergeant-Major Tonel followed him, and Dicken told us what we needed to know. We were clearly besieged by the huge Mexican force which was actually supposed to be attacking and seizing the huge supply convoy that we had been sent back to protect, therefore, every minute, every hour that the Mexicans wasted on attacking us in our entrenched position, and at great cost to themselves, was time bought for the convoy to make it safely to Puebla. All we had to do was give up our lives to ensure that it did. That might sound a high price, but to us, as Legionnaires, it was our job, it's what we had signed on to do, and we were all more than ready to go down fighting. C'est la Legion!

Jimmy often spoke later of things that I said or that he or Dicken had said during the battle at Camerone. I don't really remember saying anything other than agreeing to the oath. I probably did speak to or reassure my friends as we fought for our lives, but all the while I was fixed on the enemy and on killing them – any other considerations were secondary.

We sang that song about the Black Pudding or the Blood Sausage that we had been singing in camp, not long after Danjou's first parley with the Mexican officer, in fact, I believe that was our signal to the enemy that we had refused their terms. Jimmy and I's skill at building had helped shore up some of the bigger gaps in the walls, now it was the Mexicans who had to find a way to get us out.

I remember it was hot, even more unbearably hot than usual , and we were running low on water by late morning. After we had serenaded the Mexicans with 'Le Boudin', a vicious fire-fight began. The Mexicans had many breech loading or repeating Spencer and Sharps rifles, with much greater rates of fire than our MLE rifled-muskets, but our weapons were more deadly – every Mexican we hit was either killed , or incapacitated. We were the better shots too, but their sheer volume of fire kept our heads down a lot and began to take its toll on our numbers – we were killing a lot of Mexicans as we loaded and fired, loaded and fired, but each one of us that they managed to hit was a man we could not afford to lose. They could afford casualties, we couldn't.

Another battalion of Mexican infantry arrived, and soon the Mexicans were alternating between trying to storm us, and trying to drown us in bullets – but they couldn't do both at once! Still they came on, they lost many, we lost few, and their tactics never changed.

Then, at about mid-day, I was hit, and knocked flying backwards onto my arse. It wasn't a serious wound, just a bullet-slice at my shoulder, but as I fell, over came Captain Danjou with his Lefaucheux revolver to take my place, just as he had bravely been doing all over our line whenever someone had went down. It was then that our brave, one handed captain fell. One of the Mexicans, who had been hiding out of sight in the upper floor of the hacienda, fired a bullet down through Danjou's throat and into his chest. He died within moments. As I got back to my feet, I saw that the two Belgian lads who'd been firing at the upper floor were both dead, so, angry at the loss of my captain, I reloaded, aimed at the balcony, and plugged that bastard who killed our captain, right in the face – killing him - we wouldn't be hearing from the balcony again.

I think Second Lieutenant Vilain took over command after that. The captain's death only stiffened our resolve even further, and then, about 40 minutes later, came a glimmer of hope , when we heard distant trumpets and the lookout reported a dust-cloud on the horizon. For a few minutes we thought it might be our own cavalry or the Afrancesados cavalry , or a mix of both, coming to rescue us, just like when the Chasseurs d'Afrique had rescued us at El Abeid – but it wasn't. It was just more Mexican cavalry and infantry, and even a band. Their band played a scary, haunting yet beautiful tune to us, designed to intimidate us, it was called 'the slit throat', and though it moved us, it didn't scare us at all.

Second-Lieutenant Maudet took over command at about 2pm when Vilain was shot dead, but we kept on fighting. I was so thirsty that I licked my own shoulder wound to get some moisture in my mouth. Some of the lads were drinking their own piss. Ammo was running low too, but we fought on, using cartridges from the dead fellas. We lasted then until about 5pm, I think. Maudet was summoned to surrender after another parley with the Mexicans, and he was again asked to ask US if we wanted to surrender. Again, we responded by singing loudly, that song about the Black Pudding, Tiens, Voila du Boudin…which was again, in turn, replied to, with another huge Mexican attempt to storm us, yet still we held them back, using bayonets, bullets, rifle-butts and even our bare hands. Those soldatos were fine soldiers, but they were no match for The Legion, but then, the angry Mexicans set the hacienda on fire.

Dicken had been hit by several bullets at once and was killed instantly by the volley that followed our singing, and I saw Jimmy bend down to take what I thought was a spare cartridge from his pouch.

We had to abandon the walls and take refuge in the stable. By 6pm there were only six of us left standing, Second-Lieutenant Maudet, Corporal Maine, Me, Jimmy and two other Legionnaires, and we had only one shot left each. We were surrounded by thousands of Mexicans, all baying for our blood.

For a moment, the Mexican firing stopped, as they waited to see what we would do next. I'll never forget that brief moment's silence. We had been fighting for eleven hours and the sound of gunfire had been constant and near deafening, but to tell you the truth, in battle, you don't really hear the massed gunfire until it stops – that's what makes you realise how loud it really was, when it stops.

I remember thinking that, although we were in a sticky spot, I still preferred this simple but deadly situation to all of the troubles Jimmy and me had found ourselves in before we had joined The Legion!

The rest of our comrades were all dead or seriously wounded. We had sworn not to surrender, so, led by Maudet and Maine, the six of us fired a last volley, and charged our bayonets, before rushing screaming towards the entire Mexican force.

Six men against over 3000.

Guess who won?

That's right.

Nobody.

The Mexicans fired a volley at us as we charged. One of those who charged with us was hit by so many bullets that he fell apart, for he had tried to shield Maudet, yet Maudet was still hit twice. Another one of us was hit in the head and killed instantly. That left Corporal Maine, Jimmy and me as the last three standing Legionnaires. Still, we stood defiantly, bayonets charged, ready for whatever would befall us. Hundreds of Mexican rifles and carbines were aimed at us, still hundreds more bayonets were around us like a hedge, we were ready to die, we expected to die – after all, as Legionnaires, that's what we were there for.

Just then, a Mexican colonel, who we later found out was named Cambas, spoke to Maine in French, asking 'will you surrender now?'

Maine , unbelievably, asked terms. He demanded medical assistance for Maudet, and demanded that he, me and Jimmy, keep our weapons. I couldn't believe it – three men demanding terms from 3000!

The Mexican colonel called on some NCOs and as they approached, he said to us 'to brave men such as you, one refuses nothing!'

Two of the NCOs put Maudet on a stretcher, while me, Jimmy and Maine were told to sling our rifles and fall in, surrounded by eight huge Mexican NCOs. The ordinary Mexican soldiers protested, they wanted to tear us apart for holding them up for a full eleven hours as we had, but the NCOs kept them off – if it wasn't for the Mexican officers, I think the three of us who surrendered would have been torn limb from limb.

Out of the corner of my eye I saw another Mexican colonel, who we later found out was named Milan. He was searching the inside of the hacienda and the courtyard, and looked perplexed, scratching his head in disbelief. We knew why he was perplexed, he had clearly been expecting to find hundreds of Legion bodies – instead there were barely 50. 3rd company of The Legion's 1st battalion in Mexico had now ceased to exist, thought it would no doubt live on in legend. We had been defeated tactically, but judging by the hundreds of Mexican corpses in and around the hacienda, the thousands upon thousands of used cartridge cases that littered the battlefield, and the fact that our little half company had held off this huge Mexican force, outnumbering us by at least 50-1, for a full eleven hours, we had achieved a noble strategic victory – paid for by the blood and lives of our brother Legionnaires, and that of brave Captain Danjou, the wooden-handed man who had inspired us to fight to the end. We had done our job for the day, now, the three of us, and our wounded officer and comrades, were marched off into the mountains, into captivity.

The Mexican Colonel Milan walked over to talk to Cambas, who commanded the infantry unit who were leading us into captivity. I heard him say something like-

'No son hombres , son demonios!'

'These are not men. They are Demons.

He was right.

We had fought like Demons; we were the Demons of Camerone.

C'est la Legion.

Chapter Thirty-Three – Heroes

On Thursday, April 30th, 1863, a 65- man patrol of French Foreign Legionnaires, commanded by a captain who was an amputee and used a wooden hand, was attacked by over two brigades of well-armed Mexican soldiers, at a little place called Camerone, a village on the road between Puebla and Vera Cruz.

For eleven hours, those 65 Legionnaires held off over 3000 Mexican soldiers, against odds of over 50-1.

The Legionnaires and the Mexicans fought with equal courage and ferocity, turning one little scrap of land in Mexico into a very vision of Hell. They didn't know it at the time, but the Legionnaires were making history, not only for themselves, but for The Legion, and for France. Their cause was irrelevant on the battlefield, they were attacked, so they fought back, not to save their own skins, but to uphold the honour of The Legion, and to make sure that their comrades weren't deprived of vital supplies.

For eleven hours, Mexican troops who had been sent to seize a lucrative and strategically vital supply convoy, instead found themselves trying to dislodge one of the most heroic bands of soldiers who have ever walked this earth. The Legionnaires fought and died, until only six were left, and ammunition was gone, but even then, partly in defiance, and partly because of a sacred oath sworn to their slain captain, they fixed bayonets and charged. Their enemies, who were equally valiant, admired their courage so much that they spared the survivors of the final charge. The 3rd company of the 1st battalion of The French Foreign Legion in Mexico ceased to exist that day, but took hundreds of their enemies with them. And most importantly of all, the supply convoy that they had been sent to escort made it safely through to its destination, right under the noses of the Mexicans who had been sent to seize it. The French heavy guns from the convoy later helped batter Puebla into submission, as planned. Thus the tide of the war turned in favour of France and the Afrancesados. A scanty rescue party of Legionnaires, sent back by Colonel Jeanningros, found the deserted Camerone battle scene the next day. The Mexicans had carried off their wounded and buried their own dead, but had also taken around 20 badly wounded or captured Legionnaires with them, such was their soldierly respect for their otherwise detested enemy. The dead Legionnaires had been put into a ditch together; their heroic, one-handed Captain's body had been given a guard of honour by The Mexicans. The 3rd company had passed from reality into legend, life had left them, but honour had not.

Chapter Thirty-Four - Captivity

Now, those few days after that big battle are still a bit hazy, I'm sure Mick would say the same. Mick was the only one of the two of us with a gunshot wound, though a minor one, but we had both been badly affected by thirst, exposure to the sun and , to be frank, nervous exhaustion from our exertions back at Camerone. Sheer trauma, in other words – we were Legionnaires, but we were only human.

The Mexicans took our wounded with them as they retreated to the hills, also taking the only other fit captured Legionnaire, Corporal Maine, and us, with them. After the first day , The Mexicans divided into two columns. Our wounded comrades who still lived were carried off with Colonel Milan's column, and Corporal Maine was sent along with them, presumably so that there was at least one fit 'officer' , albeit a non-commissioned one, to speak for them and to bear witness to their treatment of the seriously wounded 2nd Lieutenant Maudet.

Mick and I, on the other hand, marched with the Mexicans under Colonel Cambas , the man who had stopped the Mexican infantry from murdering us back at Camerone, for a number of days, climbing higher into Mexico's interior, walking over dry, dusty paths and a largely desolate, but strangely beautiful landscape, until we reached a village in the foothills of some mountains. I'll never forget the feeling of relief when I was finally able to lie down on a cot in one of the little huts, having taken off my heavy hobnail boots for the first time that I could remember in weeks. I'm sure Mick felt the same, judging by the 'ahhh' of relief he let out, as he too collapsed onto his own cot.

Both of us were too weak to move much, but Mexican women from the village brought us water, helped us to wash ourselves, tended Mick's wound, fed us twice a day, and even washed our uniforms for us while we recuperated.

As we had entered the village, Colonel Cambas, who by sheer luck spoke English as well as French, having actually been born in

France, had offered us a kind of 'parole' deal, even though we weren't officers.

If we handed over our treasured rifled muskets and bayonets for safe keeping, and promised not to try to escape, we would be treated like his own wounded men, and be given a limited amount of freedom in the village. Mick and I knew that it was our duty to try to escape and rejoin our battalion, but we were also pragmatic. We had no idea where we were, let alone how to get back to Vera Cruz or any other French base, and would in all likelihood either be shot whilst trying to escape, or die of thirst or heat exhaustion whilst blundering around in the Mexican wilderness. We agreed to Cambas' offer, on the condition that he let us know how our handful of wounded comrades and Corporal Maine and 2nd Lieutenant Maudet were getting on. Our long rest continued.

Cambas posted an armed guard outside our little hut, but Mick and I knew that this man was posted there for our protection, as though the soldiers were now duty bound to treat us honourably, the villagers were not. The Mexicans only sent women in to look after us. Some were beautiful young women, dark haired beauties the like of which we had never seen before, others were older, more motherly types. They didn't say much, but they made sure that we didn't want for anything. Mick and I even managed to deduce that some of the women found Mick's red hair fascinating, as they repeatedly called him 'Colorado' – though Mick at first tried to correct them by saying , in his Irish accent, 'no Colorado, soy Irlandes', pointing out that he was from Ireland, not Colorado, until we realised what the Mexican girls were actually going on about.

About a week into our captivity, Colonel Cambas returned with news of our wounded comrades. He was honest. Seven of our comrades, including 2nd Lieutenant Maudet, had been too badly wounded to survive, and had died of their wounds, despite the best attempts of the Mexican doctors to save them.

He told us that Corporal Maine was fine, as was Corporal Berg, and that they and the few other survivors would probably be exchanged for Mexican prisoners in a few weeks' time. I asked him what was to become of us, and his reply was somewhat ambiguous at first.

He said 'I haven't decided what to do with you yet, so I'm afraid you'll just have to stay here at Casa Antigua until I return. I hope to be back in a few weeks'. He was true to his word, and returned to see us just short of nine weeks later. In the interim there wasn't much that Mick or I could do except rest and regain our strength. In many ways, we were glad of the rest time, it felt like the first truly safe place to sleep in since we had lived in Edinburgh before all that trouble that had forced us to leave. During those nine weeks, we started to go outside in the village, and did our best to get to know our hosts. After a while, it didn't seem like captivity at all. During those weeks, Mick and I talked a lot, about life, about the remarkable adventure that we had been on in the last two years, and about our 'hosts' – though we never really talked much about what had happened at that place called Camerone. Then after those nine weeks, true to his word again, Colonel Cambas returned, and he had news for us.

Chapter Thirty-Five – Honourable Foe

Colonel Cambas was smoking a cigar as he entered Mick and Jimmy's hut. He was covered in dust, his uniform was splattered with blood, and to both of them, he looked to have aged about ten years.

Unsure of what to say, or indeed of his intentions, Mick asked Cambas 'are you alright, sir?'

Cambas sat down on a stool, took a long puff on his cigar, and then exhaled, before speaking.

'Well my friends, it seems that your army is made of sterner stuff than it was when we defeated it at Puebla last year. Those heavy cannons that your company diverted my brigade from seizing tipped the balance. Our Generals were unable to halt your General Forey, and your army has taken Puebla and Mexico City itself, defeating both the towns' garrisons and the relief armies that we sent to aid them. It seems that Mexico will fall, my friends.'

He took another puff on the cigar.

Mick and Jimmy were unsure of what this news meant for them. Cambas continued.

'Our army has retreated to the province of Chihuahua, along with Presidente Juarez and what was left of our country's treasury gold. We will fight on, after all, this is our country, and where else can we go?'

'I'm sorry, Colonel' said Jimmy, unsure of what else to say.

Cambas was quick to respond.

'Sorry for what, my friend? For doing your duty? You need not apologise for that. We are all soldiers, we do as we are told. This war was not of your own making. This war is just the latest episode in that argument that has plagued my country ever since we won our independence from Spain. Doubtless it will still go on long after you French leave. And believe me my friends, you will leave one day.'

Mick then spoke.

'Colonel, sir, we still don't properly understand this war. We're not sure why we're here, or why you're having a civil war. What is the cause of Mexico's big argument?'

149

'I admire your honesty' said Cambas, before he elaborated.

'The argument is simple. Some Mexicans believe that all Mexicans are equal, both in the eyes of God, and under the law. They believe that the land of Mexico belongs to the ordinary people who till and work it, regardless of race, breeding or background. Those Mexicans, Juaristas, like me, want us to have a free and liberal country, otherwise, why did we bother winning our independence from Spain in the first place, do you see?'

'Aye' said both Jimmy and Mick at the same time. Cambas continued.

'Then there are the other Mexicans. The conservatives, the nobles, the Afrancesados. They believe that Mexico should be ruled by the rich, that its people should be peasants who know their place and are kept in line by the army and governed solely by the corrupt nobility, with the church also keeping the people in line. And now we know that we are to have a foreign emperor thrust upon us by your own Napoleon III and these 'conservatives'. The side that I have just described is the side that you have been fighting on, my friends. I have to say, never have I seen soldiers fight so well for a cause so unworthy. Doesn't that trouble you at all?'

Jimmy and Mick both stared at the ground. They knew the colonel was right, and they knew that he knew that they knew he was right too. Cambas continued.

'Back when I was a young officer and we were invaded by the Americans, a number of American soldiers, mostly Irish, but all Catholic, followed their consciences and deserted the American army to fight for Mexico, against their former country. They saw the error of their ways, and we welcomed them with open arms. They were led by a man called Jon Riley and we called them Los San Patricios'.

'The Saint Patrick's Battalion' said Mick. 'I've heard of them'.

Cambas continued.

'They were heroes to us, among the best troops in our army, but do you know what happened to them? They were all killed or captured in battle. Those who were captured by the Americans were either hanged or tortured by their former army.'

'Are you planning to form such a battalion in this war, colonel?' asked Mick. 'I'm tired of being on the wrong side.'

Jimmy glared at Mick, but it was Colonel Cambas who poured cold-water on Mick's question.

'No my friend, we are not, this is a civil war for us, with outside interference from France. There are two main reasons why we will not try to form a battalion from enemy deserters or prisoners this time. Firstly, it broke the hearts of the Mexican people when they heard what had become of the San Patricios back in 1847-48. Secondly, we don't think we'd get enough volunteers anyway. If anyone deserts from your army, it'll be to head north to the USA to join one or the other side in their civil war. Incidentally, it looks like that particular war up north will be won by the Union side – we have just heard that The Confederates' army of Lee was defeated by the Union somewhere in Pennsylvania, a place called Gettysburg, I think. That war will end soon, and when Senor Lincoln finishes that war, he'll send men and arms south to help us against you. The Americans won't tolerate a Catholic Empire on their doorstep. But that is for the future, my friends, now, we must think of today. And Irlandesa, you are not on the 'wrong side', you fought with your comrades, your Legion is your country. You're in the wrong war, but you're on the right side – your side, the side of your friends'.

Cambas then laughed to himself, the laughter getting louder, until Jimmy asked him what he was laughing about. Cambas regained his composure, and then explained himself.

'Friends, a great irony has just struck me. I was born in France; I even spent the first few years of my life and childhood there. I was born in France, yet here I am, fighting against France for my beloved country, Mexico. You two, on the other hand, were born in Scotland and Ireland, yet here you are, fighting for France against me and my country! '

Cambas resumed his laughing, this time Mick and Jimmy laughed too.

'Así es la vida' said Colonel Cambas warmly, as he stood up from the stool.

'C'est la vie' replied Jimmy.

'C'est la Legion' added Mick.

All three men laughed together once more, for those few moments that they spoke to the Colonel, they weren't enemies, they were all just soldiers, no sides, with no malice for each other and with mutual respect for one another. But Mick and Jimmy were still keen to find out their fates, so Jimmy brought Cambas's attention back to the matter in hand.

'So colonel, have you decided what you are going to do with us?' asked Jimmy.

'Yes, my Scottish friend, I have. I admire your courage, and the villagers tell me that you have behaved yourselves honourably in my absence, and no escape attempts either! I'm honoured to have fought against you, and to have been your host. I think that it would be a pity if no fit Legionnaires ever got back to France to tell the tale of our little fight at Camerone. I have received intelligence that your General Forey will be at Vera Cruz in a few days time. My men will take you there and you will be released. I'm afraid that you'll have to be blindfolded for most of the trip to Vera Cruz, for security reasons, but you can have your rifles back, and there are two things that I would like you to give to this General Forey, one is a letter. Does that sound agreeable, gentlemen?'

Mick and Jimmy nodded their agreement and thanked the kind colonel, who spoke again.

'You will leave at dawn, God bless you, Los Demonios Del Camaron!' (The Demons of Camerone).

Colonel Cambas then got up to leave the hut, but Mick called after him.

'What's the second thing we've to give to General Forey?'

'Oh yes, I also want you to give him this. A farmer found it near our little battlefield and sold it to me for 30 pesos. Here you go.'

Cambas reached into his haversack and pulled out Captain Danjou's wooden hand! Then he handed it to Jimmy, adding 'I think that your Legion may find this useful one day'. Then the colonel walked out of the hut.

Mick and Jimmy were overcome with emotion and both started to weep as they examined the wooden prosthetic hand that had belonged to their heroic captain. They wept for a good ten minutes, but they weren't just weeping for Captain Danjou – they were weeping for everyone. Captain Foster, Dicken, Roumis and all their fallen comrades. After they had composed themselves, Jimmy spoke to Mick.

'Mick, would you really have joined the Mexicans if that colonel had asked you to?'

Mick was silent for a moment, then answered.

'In an ideal world, yes I would have, Jimmy. But this is not an ideal world is it? If I'd joined them, I'd have dishonoured myself, after just winning back my honour on the field of battle. I'm a Legionnaire – we're Legionnaires, C'est la Legion.'

Jimmy smiled, then Mick spoke again.

'Besides Jimmy, I know you've got that diamond that Dicken gave you back at Camerone – How would you ever sell that safely without me to watch your back?'

Both men began to laugh, and laugh. Then Jimmy grabbed a near empty bottle of tequila that was beside their cots, took a swig, and passed the last drops in the bottle to Mick, who drank them.

Jimmy said 'Here's to Dicken, and to splitting the cash from this here diamond when we get back home. IF we get back home.'

The next morning, Mick and Jimmy were blindfolded, and had their rifles slung over their shoulders. They were then helped onto horses by what sounded like four Mexican cavalrymen, and began the journey that Colonel Cambas had promised them – back to Vera Cruz, to deliver those two items to General Forey.

Chapter Thirty-Six – Mick's Dilemma

Those weeks after the great battle at Camerone were just what Jimmy and I needed. Sure, we were prisoners of war, under guard, but we were never mistreated, as we had promised the Mexicans that we would not try to escape. We actually enjoyed, and needed the rest. We had spent so long marching back and forth from place to place, fighting here, fighting there over the last two years. It was great to have some time to rest.

My shoulder wound was looked after and was on the mend, in fact, the worst wounds that Jimmy and I had were the burns on our left hands, from all that firing back at that little hacienda of Camerone.

The senoritas who brought us water were in most cases, beautiful, even though they seemed oddly fascinated by my red hair. The senoras were equally attentive, if a little less pleasing on the eye, but that was made up for by their cooking. For those few weeks of captivity, life was strangely pleasant.

Casa Antigua was like no prison that I could imagine. It wasn't just the fair treatment.

After the first couple of weeks, we were allowed to mingle with the villagers and the small group of soldatos who had been left behind after Colonel Cambas had departed with his command.

Jimmy seemed a bit nervous when we socialised with the people, but I was in my element. They had plenty of tequila, which was most enjoyable, their food was simple but satisfying, and above all, they were like us – ordinary people, workers, farmers, builders, cooks and hunters. I have to say, I felt more empathy with them than Jimmy did. Jimmy respected them, I grew to love them. It helped that we were higher in the hills, where the air was still hot and dry, but we also enjoyed some cool, welcome mountain breezes, unlike on that horrible coastal plain where we had served with The Legion. The culture of the ordinary Mexicans spoke to my heart too. Their fandangos and ballads reminded me of the old folk music back in Ireland, as did the distant chime of cathedral bells that we often held.

I even confessed my sins for the first time in God-knows how long, and was given absolution by the visiting Priest, Padre Luna.

Part of me hoped that we would just stay at this village forever, and become Mexicans, and live a free life of honest toil, good companionship and a Godly existence. Those nine weeks or so were bliss.

For a time, it seemed that we had escaped the war, then one day, Colonel Cambas returned, with what looked like half of the men that he had left Casa Antigua with nine weeks earlier. He looked different – dust covered, still in full-kit and, well, just generally exhausted. Then when he spoke, I experienced mixed emotions such as I had rarely felt before. He told us that 'our' army, The French and their Mexican Afrancesados allies, had crushed the Mexican 'Juarista' Republican forces, taking not only Puebla, but also Mexico City itself, and in the process had defeated all attempts by the Mexicans to come to the aid of those cities. France was winning, The Legion was winning, and that made me and Jimmy proud.

On the same hand, I felt a little bit sad, sad that I had helped to contribute to the downfall of Mexico's rightful people's government, and had by my actions contributed to the impending installation of a foreign puppet European monarch on a people who clearly didn't want one ,and hadn't even been asked if they did. When Cambas spoke to us about the San Patricios and what they had did for Mexico back in the days when it was the USA's turn to bully Mexico, for a few moments I hoped with all of my Irish heart that he was going to ask me and Jimmy to join a similar, new force raised along the same lines.

The Colonel was quick to point out that no such force was planned, and was just as quick to point out to me that I was only a soldier doing my duty, and should feel no guilt for doing my duty and watching my comrades' backs. He was right too, Jimmy and I weren't on the wrong side, we were just in the wrong war.

From what Cambas said, we could tell that Mexico's army was on the back-foot, but Jimmy and I also knew how unpopular foreign wars could become back in Europe if they went on for too long, and that, with the threat of American interference also on the horizon, would eventually lead the Republican 'Juarista' Mexicans to victory over the conservative Afrancesados and their European puppet monarch.

It was just such a shame that so much blood-letting would go on until it was all finished.

In the last two years or so I had been on three continents, fought in battles, traversed a mighty ocean, and seen my friends, family and comrades die along the way. Jimmy too, had seen so much in so little time. Before Cambas returned, we had already come to the joint conclusion that this was a fight for Mexico – liberals v conservatives, and that the rest of the world should stay out of it. The glimmer of a thought of joining the Mexican side had appealed to me, but at the end of the day, I was still a Legionnaire, a soldier of France, and The Legion was now my country. Besides, I didn't think Jimmy would have joined the Mexicans even if I had, and who would look after my most trusted copain if I had left? We also had that secret diamond to sell, one day.

By joining The Legion, we had been trying to redeem our honour. Neither of us was totally sure if we had yet achieved this, but we knew that we had fought honourably, and perhaps that was the same thing?

When Colonel Cambas told us that we were being sent back to Vera Cruz, unharmed, and with Captain Danjou's hand and a message for General Forey in our possession, we were ultimately relieved, yet sad to be saying goodbye to the little village of Casa Antigua and its simple, wonderful people. The blindfolds for the journey weren't so nice, but they were necessary, though Jimmy and I had already agreed to 'forget' the name of the village that we had been 'prisoners' at, as they had treated us so fairly.

I don't remember much about the blindfolded journey back to Vera Cruz, our guards didn't say much at all. Within a few days, somehow, Jimmy and I were waiting outside a large white tent on the outskirts of Vera Cruz, about to meet our supreme commander for the first, and only time. He called us both into the tent and ordered us to attention…

Chapter Thirty-Seven –

Invisible Demons

Jimmy and Mick stood bolt-upright in the tent. Most of their kit was gone, and their rifles had been taken from them when they had been handed over to the Afrancesados Mexican cavalry who had performed the prisoner exchange. Asides that, both of their uniforms were immaculate, the Mexican women back at Casa Antigua having did their best to clean them up. Both men still had light burn wounds to their left hands, from gripping their rifles' muzzles at Camerone. The tent was large, but there were only two officers present, and one Sergeant-Major, who was clearly there to act as a scribe for the proceedings.

The extravagant, immaculate uniforms of the two high ranking officers and the NCO still contrasted greatly with the modest appearance of Mick and Jimmy. Both men recognised the second high-ranking officer as Colonel Jeanningros, commander of The Legion's contingent. The other senior officer , stout and with a huge moustache, was General Forey, who was the first to speak.

'So, Legionnaires, I trust that you were treated honourably in your captivity? You were not harmed in any way?'

'No, Sir' answered Jimmy and Mick. Forey continued.

'And where exactly were you held prisoner? What was the name of the place? Where is it?'

'Don't know, sir' was the reply from both of them. Forey persisted.

'That is a pity, as if you had been able to tell me I'd have sent a cavalry squadron up to raze the place to the ground tomorrow. No matter, you are back now, mes enfants. I give you congratulations on your freedom, and on your courage at Camerone, courage which may well save your hides!'

Jimmy spoke.

'What do you mean, sir? We did our duty, then we were taken prisoner. What have we done wrong?'

Colonel Jeanningros then looked at Forey, and then spoke to them.

'It is good to see you alive mes enfants, I saw that slaughterhouse back at Camerone, you are lucky to be here.'

'We are, sir' said Jimmy, 'in fact we-

'Don't interrupt me , Scotsman. I say you are lucky to be here. Also lucky to have been living the high life among the enemy for these last eight or so weeks, and no escape attempt, why was that, Legionnaire?'

Jimmy was a bit surprised by his colonel's tone, but composed himself and answered, slightly untruthfully, but without telling any real lies.

'Mon Colonel, we were taken prisoner. We had no idea where we were, they blindfolded us. We gave our parole and our word as Legionnaires that we would attempt no escape as long as they treated us honourably.'

'And did they treat you honouably? I'll bet they did, women, tequila, tortillas, yes mes enfants, you've had a right holiday, haven't you?' said Colonel Jeanningros, in an accusing tone.

Both Legionnaires said nothing, then General Forey spoke.

'Consorting with the enemy. Neglecting the opportunity to escape, even holding cosy chats with high-ranking enemy colonels, yes mes enfants, we hear things here at HQ, sometimes very strange things. Those Mexicans who delivered you back to us told our Mexicans everything. What have you got to say to that?'

'Nothing, mon General' answered both men, beginning to feel very scared. Nothing was more terrifying for a Legionnaire than the wrath of his superior.

Jeanningros then spoke.

'So boys, what are these two items in that little sack the Mexicans gave us?'

'A letter for the general, sir, and Captain Danjou's wooden hand, found by a farmer on the battlefield' said Mick.

'Ah yes, delivering enemy dispatches too, it's not looking good for you is it, mes enfants?' said Jeanningros.

Mick and Jimmy stood silent for a moment. Jimmy stared at his boots. They were sure that they were for the penal battalion, or maybe even execution, as they were on active service and the law allowed for it.

General Forey then stood up and spoke.

'We don't think very highly of Legionnaires who consort with enemies, withhold vital intelligence from their own officers, abandon their equipment, keep their uniforms in poor order and then become insubordinate with their superiors, do we colonel?'

'No we don't, sir' agreed Colonel Jeanningros.

The two senior officers then looked at each other, grave expressions on their faces. General Forey then ordered the thus-far silent Sergeant Major to go and fetch 'the guard', and the little man left the tent.

Mick and Jimmy were terrified, arrest was looming.

For a time, silence hung in the air.

Then General Forey started to snigger, and then to laugh, and Colonel Jeanningros joined him, both men erupting into loud, boisterous laughter.

Jimmy and Mick still stood in front of them, unsure what would happen next. Eventually, Mick could take no more tension, and asked 'what have we done wrong?'

General Forey's answer was decisive.

He leapt over his desk and embraced both Jimmy, and Mick, then Colonel Jeanningros did the same, both senior officers beaming and smiling as they did so, and as they did, the Sergeant-Major re-entered the tent, not with a prisoner guard, but with a tray, containing a bottle of wine and five cups. The two senior officers sat down again, and Jeanningros ordered Mick and Jimmy to stand at ease. The Sergeant-Major finished pouring five generous cups of wine, and gave them to the two Legionnaires and the two officers, keeping one for himself.

'Thank you, sir' said Jimmy and Mick in unison.

Colonel Jeanningros then proposed a toast, to The Legion, to France, to the heroes of Camerone, and to Captain Danjou. All five men in the room drank the toast.

General Forey then spoke , at length.

'Gentlemen, please forgive our little joke. We are delighted to see you alive, two more surviving heroes of Camerone. May God bless you and your fallen comrades. We salute you. Your actions, and those of your brave captain and your company, saved the supply convoy and got the big guns to Puebla, your heroism has almost won us this war. I've just read that 'dispatch' that your amigo Colonel Cambas sent back with you, would you like to know what it says?'

'Yes, sir' said both Legionnaires. Forey continued by reading from the note.

'These two Legionnaires that I return to you behaved with great honour and gave us no further intelligence, they are demons, not men, and you should be proud of them. But remember, General Forey, you can send ten million Legionnaires to the sacred soil of Mexico, and you will still never defeat us, unless you are prepared to stay and eat tortillas for the next thousand years'.

'What do you think about that?' Asked Forey.

Mick and Jimmy were both relieved that their earlier 'grilling' had merely been an officers' prank.

They said nothing, they didn't know what to say. Forey spoke again.

'Well, Colonel Jeanningros, what are we to do with such men as these, men who when numbering less than seven with their copains, charge with bayonets against 3000 Mexican soldiers?'

Jeanningros then spoke.

'Well , sir, we can't send them back to their company, now that their company only exists in the newspapers and the history books.'

Forey agreed, then spoke directly to the two relieved, if a tad puzzled, Legionnaires.

'Look, mes enfants, you deserve every medal that we can possibly give you. However, I can't just have you re-assigned to another company afterwards; it would be shameful if two of Camerone's demons survived such an ordeal only to succumb to le Cafard or el vomito a few months later. I also need your help'.

'Sir?' asked Mick and Jimmy, again, in unison.

'You tell them, colonel' said Forey to Jeanningros, who elaborated to the two Legionnaires, and told them their immediate fate.

'Boys, Camerone has already been widely reported in the newspapers all over Mexico and North and South America, and we've already sent back our own reports to The Emperor in Paris, to

Sidi-bel-Abbes, and to Marseille. Though you two surviving that battle and the final charge is noble, we can't have anything changing the story and thus detracting from its credibility. As far as you, and the whole world are concerned, six Legionnaires made that last charge, and you two weren't among them. We can't change the names now. I'm sorry boys but that's the way it must be. C'est La Legion. Your friend Dicken, the Englishman, will be remembered though. I'm sorry boys, but we're winning this war now, Mexico is almost ours, we can risk no blemishes to the detail or chronology of our glorious conquest and to the men's morale, the legend has already been made. You are part of it, nothing can change that, we know you were at Camerone, you know you were at Camerone, even the fucking Mexicans know you were at Camerone. But no-one else must know. I realise that this may be a bitter pill for you to swallow, mes enfants, but we can sweeten things a little for you. In view of your gallantry and tenacity, you are hereby both promoted to the rank of Sergeant Major in The Legion, and you are to return to Algeria, where you will become infantry instructors to new Legion recruits, until your contract is up. Should you choose to enlist for another five years thereafter, you will both be promoted once more – IF you agree to keep silent about your actions at Camerone – you can talk ABOUT the battle, but not your being there – do you agree?'

Jimmy and Mick were shocked, a little sad, but also delighted. With their company now dead, and knowing what they now knew about the Mexican war, they were only going to give one answer, again, in unison.

'Oui, mon colonel'.

Jeanningros and Forey then shook both men's hands, and the two Legionnaires again thanked their Colonel, and the General.

General Forey had the last word.

'The day after tomorrow, you will sail back across the ocean to Oran, tomorrow, the tailor will give you your new Sergeant-Major's uniforms, and you will each be issued with a sword and a Lefaucheux Revolver, no more rifles for you, mes enfants. Good luck, gentlemen, you are truly men of honour'.

'What about tonight, sir?' Mick asked General Forey.

'Well, Chef, the pair of you can stay here drinking with we two old officers all night, or you can have one last night in Vera Cruz, getting drunk, chasing whores and beating up the locals, which is it to be?'

'I think we'll go for the whores, sir' said Jimmy.

All five men in the tent laughed, and Colonel Jeanningros threw them a decent sized bag of coin, which Mick caught, Jeanningros adding with a wink, 'back-pay -for tonight's entertainment'.

The little Sergeant Major then made Mick and Jimmy swear on the wooden hand of Captain Danjou that they would never speak of what they did at Camerone, but also that they would never forget that day either, and this they did, before saluting the senior officers, and turning, marching out of the tent.

When they got out of earshot of the tent, Mick turned to Jimmy.

'So Jimmy lad, back to Sidi for us, drill instructors eh, who'd have thought that, and Sergeant-Majors to boot!'

'Sounds good to me' answered Jimmy.

'C'est La Legion' said Mick.

'C'est la Vie' said Jimmy, and the pair of them disappeared into Vera Cruz for the night.

Sure enough, the next day, they were both promoted to Sergeant Major, and received new uniforms, swords, and Lefaucheux revolvers. Next day, they had left Mexico forever, on a troop ship filled with crippled soldiers. Talk everywhere was of Camerone, but neither Mick, nor Jimmy, said a word about it. They now faced a seven-week Atlantic voyage, hopefully a relaxing one, and both men were glad to be leaving the troubled nation of Mexico behind, a beautiful land that they both hated and loved, and would never forget.

Chapter Thirty-Eight – Napoleon's Folly

Napoleon III's grand scheme for domination in Mexico had relied on the assumption that the Confederate side would triumph in the neighbouring USA's civil war. After 1863, Confederate victory looked less-likely with every month that passed, yet Napoleon and France pressed on regardless.

After Camerone and the victories at Puebla and Mexico City, France was virtually the master of Mexico, in that it couldn't be defeated on the battlefield, and France's navy imposed an effective blockade of Mexico by sea. General Forey was promoted to Marshal after the victories of mid 1863, but was soon replaced by General Bazaine, who himself was also made Marshal Bazaine early in 1864.

Maximilian finally arrived and was crowned Emperor of The Second Mexican Empire, in April of 1864.

The French and their Afrancesados allies then found themselves fighting a prolonged anti-insurgency campaign against Juarez's tenacious Republicans, and encountered most of the same problems that foreign occupying forces have faced in others' countries before and since in history. France's Army, and its much vaunted Legion, often found itself acting almost like a reactionary fire-brigade. They could react to Mexican Juarista attacks and operations, and were the better fighting force, but more often than not, they had to return to their bases and hand back any ground that they had taken in battle, often returning to fight the Mexicans for the same piece of ground on one or more occasions.

General Bazaine's counter-insurgency campaign, though effective, was brutal, and ruthless, which was counter-productive, and led to many 'on the fence' Mexicans, and even some conservative /Afrancesados ones, flocking to Juarez's Republican side, as more and more, it became clear that to be for Juarez was to be for Mexico, and to be for Maximilian was to be for France, and for occupation by foreign soldiers. In some ways, Bazaine's tactics were too effective, as for a time they drove Juarez's forces over the Rio Grande into America, which caused further political difficulties.

Maximilian tried to please everybody, and ended up pleasing nobody. His liberal policies and reforms weren't that different from those that Juarez had already enacted or had intended to enact, which alienated many of his conservative supporters, in other words, Maximilian wasn't right-wing enough for his Mexican right-wing supporters. As the war dragged on, it became easier and easier for the 'true' Mexicans to portray Maximilian as a foreign puppet emperor whose only authority came from the legions of foreign soldiers who made up the bulk of his army, and towards the end, that's all he really was. Maximilian's regime treated many captured Juaristas as terrorists, not soldiers, executing them out of hand, and such behaviour rarely strengthens a regime – it usually destroys it.

Juarez and the Mexican liberal/republican side showed great tenacity and never gave up, but in the end, it wasn't their courage and fighting prowess that were to be the deciding factors in Mexico's 'great argument' – the deciding factors were ultimately political.

From early 1864, France recruited tens of thousands of Legionnaires and soldiers specifically for the Mexican campaign, but many thousands of them only really enlisted to get a free passage across the Atlantic, then on arrival in Mexico, promptly went on 'promenade' to the United States, never to be seen again. Most of the initial Legion force of veterans that was sent to Mexico early in 1863 was by then dead, or sent home wounded. Only a few hundred of the original 1500 strong Legion force ever saw Europe again.

France even had to rely on help from other European powers to bolster Maximilian's army. Over 6000 troops from his native Austria fought in Mexico, as did 1500 Belgians, and towards the end of the war, around 1800 former American Confederate soldiers. Maximilian was even given a battalion of Egyptian soldiers to aid him in Mexico. In the end, these additional deployments to supplement the near 40,000 French troops who had served there, were to be in vain.

By 1865, the Mexican intervention was becoming very unpopular with the ordinary people of France, and even more unpopular in the neighbouring United States, where, after Lee's surrender to Grant at Appomattox in April 1865, policy changed from one of covert assistance and diplomatic persuasion on the part of the Americans, who supported Juarez's republicans, to threats of open war against France and even threats of an American invasion of Mexico to get rid of the French and their allies once and for all. Sympathetic Americans raised some $18m dollars in bonds for Juarez's side, and America even donated 30,000 rifles from its Baton-Rouge arsenal to aid Juarez and the republicans.

America may have been Mexico's enemy in the past, but in the 1860's, ironically, her support was crucial to Mexico's ultimate fight for freedom from foreign interference.

Napoleon III, under pressure at home to end the war, and threatened with war with the United States – who at the time had a huge, well-equipped and experienced, confident army, fresh from winning its own civil war – chose to end the Mexican experiment, and in May 1866, French and satellite troops began to withdraw from Mexico and make their way back across the Atlantic, as did most of Maximilian's French political advisors. Though Napoleon III urged Maximilian to leave Mexico with them, for reasons unknown, he chose to remain behind to try to defend his Imperial throne. As soon as his European troops began withdrawing though, Maximilian's Mexican conservative troops began to suffer defeat after defeat at the hands of Juarez's republicans, who, with the departure of the foreign troops, now enjoyed both the initiative and a huge military superiority. Maximilian and his dwindling forces managed to hang on until early May 1867, when Maximilian was captured by the republicans, and executed by firing squad a month later, along with many of his Mexican conservative Afrancesados cronies.

Benito Juarez was again installed as president by the Mexican people, and France's intervention in Mexico was over. Mexico was free at last. Benito Juarez is perhaps the most loved political figure in Mexican history – Maximilian is one of the most reviled.

During the intervention, The French Foreign Legion fought like Lions, to the point that the Juarista republican forces avoided all contact with Legion units whenever possible, usually only encountering them when The Legion was rushed to some remote place to rescue another body of Maximilian's troops. That day at Camerone, when Mexico's finest had faced the one-handed captain and his 64 'demons', had dissuaded Juarez's soldiers from any further major attacks on The Legion. France and its allies had lost the war in Mexico, but The Legion had not lost its honour.

165

Chapter Thirty-Nine– Invisible Rewards

1876. Sidi-Bel-Abbes

The barrack square at Sidi-Bel-Abbes was packed with Legionnaires who had just completed their training. 400 men in pristine uniforms stood to attention , intently listening to a ranting NCO who roared at them a mix of violent threats and grudging encouragement. The air was as devilishly hot as ever, and the Legion flag and France's tricolour fluttered in the air on two poles above them all. A bugle sounded in the distance, but the NCO kept barking at the assembled troops. Their uniforms were much the same as ever, but now the Legionnaires carried breech-loading Le Gras rifles, which presently sat ordered by them as they stood at attention.

France's Army had suffered horrendous casualties in the war of 1870-71 between France and Prussia, and The Legion was only now, five years later, beginning to look anything like its former self.

Some Legionnaires and officers had stayed behind in Algeria as the rest of The Legion had gone off to defend France, some gladly, some grudgingly. Two Sergeant-Majors had stayed behind, and had thus missed the carnage of the war's latter stages and the fall of Paris and The Empire. They had protested their orders at the time, but Napoleon III himself had insisted that they both remain at Sidi to help oversee the NCOs who trained the new recruits, and also for another reason – he did not want either of these two men to be harmed, they were living mementoes – albeit largely unknown ones.

The Legionnaires and their officers and NCOs at Sidi were now no longer soldiers of the French Empire, but of The Third French Republic, which had eventually been established following the defeat, capture and subsequent deposition of Napoleon III after the Battle of Sedan and France's defeat by Prussia.

The 400 Legionnaires assembled on the barrack square were about to march south into the desert, to relieve a French garrison that was under siege by a force of Arabs, and thus to receive their first taste of desert warfare.

The NCO, a Sergeant-Major Arpinon, bellowed reminders to the men and then had had them sing La Marseillaise, then, as the singing stopped he was interrupted.

'I'll take over from here, Chef'

'Oui, mon Capitaine' said the Sergeant-Major, as two figures replaced him on the steps that he had been using as a makeshift podium from which to make himself heard.

The two figures were both dressed in the uniforms of Legion Captains, wearing red breeches instead of white, and with red and gold epaulettes on their uniforms. At each man's side hung a revolver and a sabre.

The taller man was six feet tall and had brown hair and a facial scar, and looked to have been sunbathing for most of his adult life, such was the tan of his skin. The second man was only four inches shorter, but had red hair and was more wiry and strong looking. He too had dark skin, a sure sign of many years spent in the blazing sun. Both men were in their mid 30's.

The man with the scar loudly addressed the Legionnaires first.

'Mes enfants, I am Captain Reid of the headquarters battalion, the man standing beside me is Captain Warfield, also of the headquarters battalion here at our glorious fortress of Sidi-Bel-Abbes. You march to meet the enemy. Now, your own officers have already briefed you and will meet you at the main gate. In the meantime, I have something to tell you.'

The Legionnaires assembled in front and below the two captains stood like statues, in silence, filled with a mix of dread and exhilaration. The Captain continued.

'During this march, or in the weeks to come, many of you will decide that you don't wish to be soldiers of France anymore. Most of you will be good soldiers, but some of you will try to run away. If you run away, you not only risk your own life – you also put in jeopardy the lives of your copain, your comrades in arms, your brothers. Yes, some of you will try to run away. No man in our

167

command has ever succeeded! If the Arabs don't get you, thirst will. If thirst doesn't get you, the desert will. If the desert doesn't get you, The Legion will, and if The Legion doesn't get you…I WILL'.

'And if he doesn't get you, I sure as hell will!' boomed the other, red-haired, shorter Captain, sternly adding 'I don't know which is worse.'

The Legionnaires assembled stood motionless and silent, and had clearly gotten the message.

'Sergeant-Major, take these men to their officers at the main gate' said the red-haired captain to the NCO, who soon had the men formed into columns of fours.

As the column of Legionnaires made to march out of the barrack square, the two Captains began to sing, loudly, from their elevated position on the steps, and after the first two lines, the Legionnaires joined in, and continued singing the song until they were just dots on the horizon to the men left back at Sidi.

'Tiens, voilà du boudin, voilà du boudin, voilà du boudin
Pour les Alsaciens, les Suisses et les Lorrains,
pour les Belges y en a plus,
pour les Belges y en a plus,
ce sont des tireurs au cul
pour les Belges y en a plus,
pour les Belges y en a plus,
ce sont des tireurs au cul
Tiens, voilà du boudin, voilà du boudin, voilà du boudin
Pour les Alsaciens, les Suisses et les Lorrains!'

'You know Jimmy, I always kinda thought that song would catch on' said Mick to his fellow Captain.

'Aye Mick, it is sort of infectious. It sounds so much better now though, doesn't it?' said Jimmy.

'No' said Mick. 'I always preferred the Mexican version, mon copain.'

'When were you in Mexico?' said Jimmy to Mick, with a wink.

Both men laughed loudly, and headed to the officer's mess.

Captain James Reid and Captain Michael Warfield spent the rest of the evening having a farewell drink with fellow officers, telling war stories and singing 'Le Boudin'. They were due for discharge, having completed fifteen years' service in The Legion. Both men, in their mid 30's, looked forward to going home, and to collecting their pensions. In the many years that they had been back at Sidi, they had never once spoken of being at Camerone. Everyone they met knew that they were heroes of the Mexican war, but that was all that they ever knew. C'est la Legion.

Chapter Forty - Captains

Jimmy and I were assigned to permanent duties at Sidi-Bel-Abbes as soon as we arrived back from Mexico. We were drill sergeants, charged with turning raw, new recruits into Legionnaires, and we loved it. We were hard but we were fair, we had learned from Lejaune and Dupre how to be NCOs, and how not to be NCOs. Life became relaxed, almost tolerable, but that fight at Camerone in Mexico was never far from our minds, though we only ever spoke of it in private. In late 1870 we were amazed and delighted to be promoted lieutenants, but our joy was tempered by the fact that we had been selected to stay behind at Sidi-Bel-Abbes while the greater number of The Legion sailed back to defend France from the Prussians. It was clear that someone, somewhere, in the high command, wanted us kept alive.

Both of us had re-signed for another five years in The Legion, in 1866 and again in 1871, whereupon they promoted us both to Captain. We were distraught to see so few of our comrades return to Algeria from the great war against Prussia, but we had little time to grieve – we had recruits to train. Then in 1876, our enlistments ran out once more. We had served fifteen years, fifteen damn years! We qualified for a pension and were given service medals by France's new Republican Government. All that trouble back in Edinburgh, Paris and Ireland seemed like an age ago, but now, at last, we were both in a position to go home and confront it.

The clerk back at Sidi had rectified the error with our names when we re-enlisted back in 1866, and to tell you the truth, it took a few months for Jimmy and I to get used to being called by our real names again.

I tell ya, Private Jimmy and Private Mick, and later as Sergeant-Majors, the Scotsman and the Irishman, how much more stereotypical could our noms de guerre have been?

We decided that when we left The Legion, we would take up the offer of French citizenship, but would do so under our real names. A ten-Franc bribe was all it took to sort that out. Both of us kept our uniforms and even our side-arms, as we thought that they may come in useful at some point, and we were right.

Looking back on those years now, sometimes I can't believe that we did the things that we did. We may have lost our honour in Ireland and Scotland, and been shamed by being robbed in France at that diamond merchant's, but The Legion had changed everything for us. We had been part of a 65 man band of brothers that had fought an entire army to a standstill for a whole day. We had fought on two continents, suppressed an Arab Jihad uprising, and, perhaps most precious to our hearts, we had kept our oath to that mysterious, heroic one handed captain back at that place called Camerone. We had also helped to train thousands of new Legionnaires, and had learned so much about the world, and above all, we had never, ever given up, no matter what befell us. 1876 saw us return to civilian life and we were no longer soldiers, but in our hearts we would always be Legionnaires, and that would stand us in good stead for anything else that life was to throw at us. C'est la Legion! All that me and my friend Jimmy Reid had to do now was to decide where to go next...

Chapter Forty-One – Reflections

Those days in The Legion I will never forget. I don't miss the tedious marches, the short-water rations, or the enemy soldiers trying to kill me and my friends in a variety of different ways, but I miss being a Legionnaire, and part of me will always be a Legionnaire. I too was relieved to get my 'own' name back in 1866. Training those recruits at Sidi for the rest of my career wasn't what I had expected, but then again, I had never expected to traverse three continents, sail a great ocean twice or to fight in one of the most heroic actions of all time. The memory of Captain Danjou and our other slain comrades has been a source of both pride and sorrow to me ever since those fateful days back in Mexico in 1863. My friend Michael Warfield and I joined the French Foreign Legion because we thought that we had lost our honour, looking back, I don't think that we had, we were partly running away from ourselves, but in The Legion, we found ourselves, we found purpose, pride, comradeship and self-respect. As we look back on those days in The Legion from the relative safety of our firesides in Edinburgh, surrounded by our friends and families, we take stock. What is honour? I'll tell you. Honour is being true to your friends, standing up to those who try to abuse you, standing up for those who cannot protect themselves, and looking after your family. As for honour in war, as with glory, it only truly exists in survival and in not deserting your comrades. Michael Warfield and I redeemed our honour, we were Legionnaires once, and proud, we marched or we died, The Legion was our country, and we were The Demons of Camerone. Honour could demand no more from us.

Chapter Forty-Two – Unfinished Business

After discharge in 1876, Michael Warfield and Jimmy Reid headed first for Paris, still wearing their Captains' uniforms and carrying their side-arms. They visited a pawnbroker's in Montmartre, and the elderly, frail old man who ran the shop with who looked like his son didn't recognise them.

Jimmy showed the pawnbroker the diamond that he had carried hidden on his person for 13 years, ever since a dying Dicken had told him to take it at Camerone. The pawnbroker was impressed, and offered a tidy sum for the precious stone , but Jimmy informed the pawnbroker that he thought the offer was derisory, and both men turned to leave the shop. The old man called out to them, claiming that he 'might know someone' who would buy the stone at a better price, if they were prepared to wait for an hour. Jimmy and Mick agreed, and the old man sent his son off to find the prospective 'buyer'.

Sure enough, Markov, the old crook who had robbed Mick, Jimmy, Dicken and Roumis back in 1861, walked into the shop an hour later, flanked by two huge, ogre-esque thugs. He too, did not recognise Mick or Jimmy, and they exchanged pleasantries, before Markov asked to see the diamond that he had been summoned to the shop to buy.

As he examined the stone, the colour drained from Markov's face, and he looked left, and then right, at his two henchmen, saying nothing. He looked at the stone again, then asked Jimmy where it had come from.

'Peter Dicken told us to give it to you' said Jimmy, just as the ominous sound of Mick cocking his revolver filled the room with tension. Jimmy then drew his own revolver, and gestured the old pawnbroker and his son into the corner of the shop, and took two paces back, so that he and Mick could easily cover all five of them.

'Interesting situation, isn't it, Monsieur Markov?' said Jimmy.

Markov knew that he had been 'had', and that there was nothing he could do. No-one would take his word against that of two decorated French officers, and he knew it. He also knew that his two 'ogres' stood no chance in a fight against these men, and still more urgently on his mind, was the nagging thought that this situation might actually see him caught for the dozens of other robberies that he and his thugs had pulled over the years, using this shop. He had no option, like in a Grimm's Fairy Tale, he had at last been defeated by his own greed.

'So, Legionnaires, what do you want?' said Markov, through gritted teeth, his shoulders slumping.

Jimmy made him turn out his pockets, and as he did, a wad of banknotes fell to the ground, contained by a metal clip. Jimmy picked up the wad, and to his astonishment, found there to be nearly 5000 Francs in 50 Franc notes! Jimmy re-clipped the wad and tossed it to Mick, who looked at it, smiled, and then exclaimed 'Well Mr. Markov, you've paid your debts at last!'

One of Markov's ogres growled and took a step towards Mick, but then Jimmy cocked his own revolver, and the sound of that made the man freeze in his place. Jimmy then ushered Markov, the two ogres, the shopkeeper and his son into the shop's storeroom, then locked it from the outside, despite their protests.

They had got Dicken's money back, or at least some of it, a tidy enough sum to be going home with, and they still had Dicken's diamond, and best of all, they hadn't spilled a drop of blood in doing so. They left the shop, giggling like schoolboys, the angry thumping coming from the inside of the shop's storeroom being the last thing that they heard before stepping outside.

'What now, Mick?' said Jimmy.

'Ireland first, then Edinburgh, is that alright with you, mon copain?' he replied.

'Oui' said Jimmy, and the pair of them strolled off into Paris's bustling streets, heading for the railway station that would see them catch a train to Brest, and then a boat to Ireland, feeling very pleased with themselves.

Chapter Forty-Three - Homecoming

Michael Warfield and Jimmy Reid led largely uneventful lives after they had gained their long awaited revenge in Paris. They were in Sligo within a month, where they soon found Mick's twin sister Siobhan, who had been married but then been widowed in all the time that Mick had been away. The Sweeney incident had been forgotten – no-one in Sligo had liked him. When Jimmy and Mick found Siobhan, she was working in a school, teaching. After a tearful reunion with Mick and a quick visit to their family's graves, Mick and Siobhan accompanied Jimmy to Scotland, back to the beautiful city of Edinburgh, where an unexpected surprise awaited Jimmy Reid.

Conscious that Edinburgh's Police might still be looking for him and Mick, Jimmy was pleased that they were both still wearing their Legion uniforms and carrying their French identification, but he needn't have worried too much.

As the three of them walked up the now completed Cockburn Street from the railway station, the very street where Mick and Jimmy had worked together when it was still just the town council's vision, the familiar smells and sights of Edinburgh came back to both men. Then, as they crested the hill and looked up the high street, they saw people, so many people; it was as if Edinburgh's population had quadrupled in their absence. As they reached the door of Reid's Ironmongers, Jimmy was relieved to see his old dad, stooped over the counter, scribbling accounts.

'Give me a minute please' said Jimmy to Mick and Siobhan.

Jimmy entered the shop on his own, the bell above the door ringing as he did so.

The old man looked up from his accounts and peered at the six-foot tall soldier in the doorway, and angrily exclaimed 'where the hell have you been ya wee shite?'

Jimmy didn't know what to say – that was a deep, deep question, but before he could answer, his father had walked around the counter to embrace his son, then he spoke.

'Got your letter by the way, son, just as well you went when you did, but all's well now my boy, no-one misses that bastard Ogilvie. Did you get our letter?'

'No dad, I didn't' said Jimmy.

Mr. Reid rolled his eyes, and then spoke. 'Oh Jesus, well, looks like I'm no the only one who's getting a surprise today eh!'

'Eh?' said Jimmy, reverting back to his Edinburgh slang with swift alacrity.

'John, come here son' shouted Mr. Reid.

Through the little door that led out to the back-room of the Reid's Ironmonger's shop, came a teenage boy, tall for his age, about fifteen years old, as far as Jimmy could tell.

'You're my dad, aren't you mister' said the boy, in a broad, if a little high pitched, Edinburgh accent.

Jimmy didn't know what to say. Then the boy spoke again, loudly.

'Mother, come through here the now, father's back!'

A flabbergasted Jimmy's eyes lit up when none other than Margaret Ogilvie came out of the store-room into the shop, tears in her eyes. She looked as beautiful as ever, older sure, but still beautiful with her long dark-brown hair and entrancing brown eyes. Jimmy looked at her, and then at the boy, John.

He was the very image of Margaret, but he also had the look of Jimmy about him, and Jimmy knew it – it was his son. He quickly calculated in his head that that was indeed the case, and , not knowing what to say, embraced them both. Joy filled his heart, and that joy was increased when he heard another female voice, an older one, in a reproachful tone, saying 'Jesus, son, do they no feed you in that bloody foreign legion?'

It was Mary, Jimmy's mother. Jimmy turned to Margaret.

'So that's why you ran away from us in London then?'

'Aye Jimmy, I had to come home, I'd only have been a burden. I've been helping your mum and dad run the shop here all these years, so has your son since he's been old enough, have you said hello to your dad yet, John?' said Margaret.

'Aye he has' said Jimmy, surprisingly calmly under the circumstances, but beaming with pride inside.

Jimmy took the time to warmly embrace them all, and thanked God that he had lived to see his family again, and for his son.

'Who's that outside , son?' asked Mary, Jimmy's mother.

'You remember Mick, don't you?' said Jimmy, before shouting to Mick and Siobhan to come into the shop.

Mick looked inquisitive, then simply said hello to everyone, and guessed the identity of the little boy correctly, before introducing Siobhan to Jimmy's family.

Mr. Reid senior then closed the shop and invited everyone upstairs for some dinner, the Warfields, the Reids, and Miss Ogilvie, got to know each other all over again, over stovies and whisky.

As it turned out, Margaret had remained single, and had battled the stigma of having a child with no father, though thankfully, the fact that Jimmy had been away in the army had been enough to quash any nasty gossip, and besides, she had lived respectfully with Jimmy's parents, and even converted to Episcopalianism, meaning that no-one batted an eyelid about her circumstances.

Jimmy and Margaret's son was handsome, clever and funny, just like his mother and father, and was soon calling Mick 'Uncle' and Siobhan 'Auntie'.

Mick and Jimmy lived out the rest of their days in Edinburgh, in a life of fantastic normality, free from bullets, bayonets, orders, disease and le Cafard. Jimmy and Margaret soon married, while Mick and Siobhan both also found suitable spouses among the Cowgate Irish community, and were married to their new spouses in The Cowgate's St Patrick's Church. Mick and Jimmy hired a load of young fellas from The Cowgate and got the old building firm going again, and made a great success of it, and helped to drag many of the Cowgate's Irish families out of poverty as a result. They re-named the building firm 'Capital City Service'.

Mick, his sister Siobhan and their respective spouses became involved in an exciting new project, a sports club that had been formed to give Edinburgh's Irish a chance to play football together against other Scottish teams. Jimmy, Margaret and wee John often accompanied them to the matches at The Meadows, and then at Newington and later in Leith to cheer on this new Irish football team from Edinburgh, they played in green and white hooped shirts, and they were called Hibernian, named for the Latin name for Ireland.

Neither Mick, Jimmy or their families ever had to worry about money, what with their Legion pensions, the Francs that they had reclaimed in Paris, and especially after they sold Dicken's diamond, ironically, to a French pawnbroker in Leith one day.

As with all good stories, they all lived happily ever after.

Jimmy only ever spoke to Mick about what had happened at Camerone, and in The Legion, no-one else, except once, when Margaret coaxed some information out of him after a particularly intimate moment in bed together, one night after Hibernian had defeated Heart of Midlothian, and Margaret never repeated the tale to anyone.

Chapter Forty-Four –

Le Boudin And The Hibs

Michael Warfield and Jimmy Reid had been on a great adventure. They had joined the finest fighting force that the world has ever seen, and fought in its most famous battle , and lived to tell the tale – albeit just to each other. They had seen and did things that seemed impossible, even to them, the older that they got. They had fled Scotland and Ireland because they had killed people for understandable reasons and thus lost their honour, yet they had redeemed their honour by killing people for dubious, often confusing reasons on the field of battle. They had found peace at last in Edinburgh though.

By 1880 both of them were fathers and husbands, as well as business partners, but they never forgot their roots. To the people of Edinburgh they were just Mick and Jimmy, the friendly builders, but they never forgot that once, not so long ago, they had redeemed their lost honour by becoming soldiers in France's Foreign Legion, and being part of that tiny half-company, who at a place called Camerone in Mexico in 1863, had fought off an entire army for nearly twelve hours. They were ordinary men again now, and glad to be so, but the day that they became The Demons of Camerone was theirs forever.

Every year in April, on or near the anniversary of Camerone, Mick and Jimmy would set aside one day, usually a day that Hibernian Football Club was playing on. The lovely Margaret, Jimmy's beloved wife, would make a pot of soup for them, and then leave Mick and Jimmy to eat it along with some bread and coffee, just like the daily meal that they had enjoyed, or sometimes endured, in The Legion, then the two men would go off to watch the match, and whether Hibs won or lost, on that night they would get really drunk on cheap, pinard style red wine, sing songs, remember fallen comrades and reminisce about the days that they had worn the uniform of The Legion. Every Hogmanay , Jimmy and Mick and their extended families and workmates would insist on singing a little song about black pudding just after the bells. Everyone in their company knew the catchy song and joined in, despite the fact that only Mick and Jimmy knew the song's true meaning, for in Edinburgh, only they were The Demons of Camerone.

'Tiens, voilà du boudin, voilà du boudin, voilà du boudin
Pour les Alsaciens, les Suisses et les Lorrains,
pour les Belges y en a plus,
pour les Belges y en a plus,
ce sont des tireurs au cul
pour les Belges y en a plus,
pour les Belges y en a plus,
ce sont des tireurs au cul
Tiens, voilà du boudin, voilà du boudin, voilà du boudin
Pour les Alsaciens, les Suisses et les Lorrains!'

The vital moment when Danjou's Number 3 Company abandoned their exposed square in the open and made a courageous fighting withdrawal to the shelter of the Hacienda at Camerone, where they made their historic, valiant last stand. Illustration by May Yang, 2014.

Captain Jean Danjou, the iconic hero of Camerone, complete with his wooden hand, and wearing a sombrero, as many French soldiers did in camp while in Mexico – though he was wearing his Kepi at Camerone. Danjou had lost his hand in 1853 after his rifle had misfired and exploded, yet he battled his disability, and was able to remain in the service after proving that he could still handle his horse's reins and his weapons. He had fought in The Crimea and at Magenta, as well as in North-Africa, prior to his fateful deployment to Mexico. He was 35 years old when he was killed. In reality, his wooden hand was actually discovered on the Camerone battlefield by a Mexican farmer named Ramirez in 1865, who, realising its significance, sold it to some of Maximilian's Austrian troops after they arrested him, and the wooden-hand is now France's Army's most prized possession. Illustration by Martin Symmers, 2014.

A typical Mexican Juarista soldier, with his basic white 'soldato' uniform, sombrero and equipment. Not all of Juarez's men were dressed in this manner – some wore the old, more garish uniforms of Mexico's army, while others simply wore their own clothes. Illustration by Chris Wainwright, 2014.

Corporal Maine of 'number three company', one of only three Legionnaires left on their feet after the battle and final charge at Camerone, and the NCO who defiantly demanded terms from The Mexicans, rather than submit to unconditional surrender. Here he is with standard Legion uniform and weapon of the day. During The Mexican Campaign, Legionnaires were encouraged to grow beards and to smoke cigars, in a futile attempt to stave off the tropical diseases that had decimated their numbers. Illustration by Chris Wainwright, 2014.

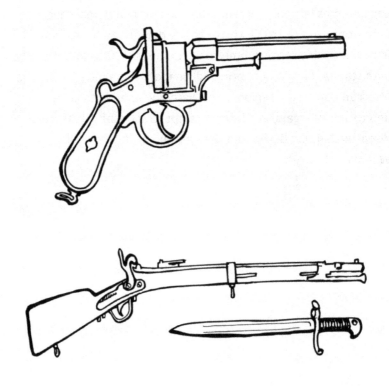

The Legion's iconic weapons of the Mexican Intervention, and of Camerone. The enlisted men's' MLE 1859 rifled-musket, with sword-bayonet, and the Lefaucheux M1858 revolver, which was used primarily by officers and by French cavalry – what there was of it. Illustration by Chris Wainwright, 2014.

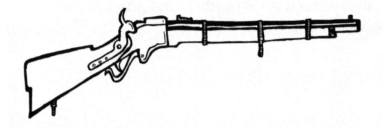

The Spencer Repeating Rifle. Thought it had a reduced range, this breech-loading lever-action weapon could be fired up to 20 times per-minute, as it was fed by a seven-shot tube magazine. Again, this was one of the weapons used by The Mexicans at Camerone. Like the Sharps Rifle, it gave its firer a huge advantage over an opponent who was armed with a muzzle-loader. Illustration by Chris Wainwright, 2014.

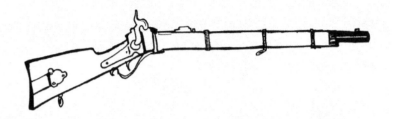

The Sharps breech-loading rifle. Though also a single-shot weapon, this had a much greater volume of fire than the rifled-musket, and was one of the weapons used by The Mexicans at Camerone. The original design used paper cartridges. Capable of firing ten rounds per-minute, as opposed to the three or four per-minute that the French MLE was capable of. As with all breech loaders, it gave the infantryman the edge over an opponent who was armed with a muzzle-loader, as the breech-loader could be easily reloaded from a prone position. Illustration by Chris Wainwright, 2014.

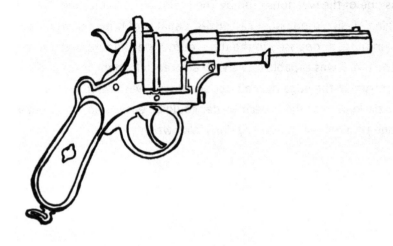

The French Lefaucheux M1858 revolver, the same model used by Captain Danjou, and Second- Lieutenants Villain and Maudet at Camerone. A six-shot sidearm that used self-contained metallic cartridges – the first of its type to be issued by any national government. Popular with Legion Officers and with France's Navy, but officers in France's regular army had to buy one at their own expense if they wanted one, unless they were in the cavalry. 12,000 of these fine, deadly weapons, were also used in The American Civil War. Illustration by Chris Wainwright, 2014.

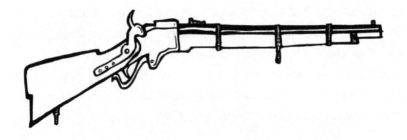

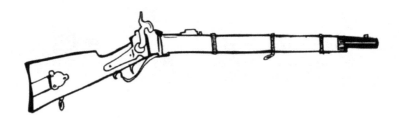

The Carbine versions of the Spencer Rifle (top) and Sharps Rifle. They were shorter barrelled models, which made them easier to use from horseback or in confined spaces. Most Mexican cavalrymen at Camerone were armed with either of these weapons, and either a sabre or a lance. Though great for a dismounted fire-fight or for mounted combat, this combination of weapons was actually a hindrance to Mexican cavalry at Camerone when they dismounted and tried to storm the Hacienda, as the carbines had no bayonets, and obviously they couldn't shoot anyone with their swords and lances. However, not all of The Mexican troops had breech-loaders - some Mexican infantry were armed just like The Legionnaires, with rifled-muskets and bayonets, and some of the irregulars even had old smoothbore weapons. The Sharps Carbine was most famously used by Buford's Union Cavalry at Gettysburg in 1863 during America's civil-war, where on the first day of the battle, its increased rate of fire helped Buford's two brigades of dismounted cavalrymen fatally delay a whole division of Confederate infantry, who were armed with slower, muzzle-loading rifled muskets. Illustration by Chris Wainwright, 2014.

The shorter version of the MLE rifled-musket, issued primarily to French Dragoons and mounted infantry, and also used by some Mexicans. Asides its barrel length, it differs very little from the main French infantry and Legion MLE 1859, and even has the same sword-bayonet. Later, towards the end of the Mexican Intervention, it was adapted into a breech loader, making it easier to use from horseback. Illustration by Chris Wainwright, 2014.

A Legionnaire bayonets a downed Mexican during the retreat back to Camerone. Illustration by John Colquhoun, 2014.

A Legionnaire having to stand on a pile of rubble in order to see over and fire over the high wall, while his comrade attempts to repair the wall. As the Hacienda was not a military building and therefore had no firing step or embrasures, its defenders, like the defenders of The Alamo back in 1836, had to fire from improvised positions, either standing on objects/rubble, or from loopholes. Illustration by John Colquhoun, 2014.

Historical & Author Note

As you may have noticed, some of my wee novel that you've just read is factual, or rather, built around real events, other parts of it came from my head. As a writer I try to tell a good story which will either entertain the reader or make them want to read more about the campaign and subject matter featured in the story, or preferably both. I'm no expert on The Legion, but the depiction of the Battle of Camerone in 1863 and most of the background information in this book regarding the French Intervention in Mexico, and The Legion itself, are all <u>mostly</u> based on fact, with a little artistic license, while the goings on in Ireland, Scotland, England, France and Algeria are mostly fictitious.

For creative purposes, I changed some names of the six men who made that crazy, defiant bayonet charge at the end of the Battle of Camerone. (Some accounts claim five charged, not six, leaving out poor Legionnaire Leonhart, who was shot dead in the final charge).The actual charge was made by 2nd Lieutenant Maudet, Corporal Maine and Legionnaires Constantin, Wenzel, Katau and Leonhart.

Only Maine, Constantin and Wenzel were still on their feet when the charge and the battle ended.

If it wasn't for the intervention of the Mexican officers after the final charge at Camerone, in all likelihood, the survivors would have been lynched by the enraged Mexican Juarista soldiers. In the end, seven of the captured or wounded Legionnaires, including Maudet, died of their injuries, despite the best efforts of the Mexican doctors. The handful of Legionnaires who survived captivity and their wounds were treated honourably, and were quickly exchanged for captured Juaristas. A story has endured that years later, after both being commissioned as officers, Corporals Berg and Maine ended up fighting a duel. I don't put much faith in that tale myself, but if it is indeed true, it's a sad tragedy.

Jimmy Reid and Michael Warfield are my own creations, their names, but not their characters, are based on good people that I know. Dicken, the Englishman, was a real Legionnaire from England who actually did fight at Camerone. As for poor Roumis, he takes his name from the derogatory name given to Legionnaires by their Arab adversaries in North Africa. 'The hated Roumis' as PC Wren brilliantly put it – it's ironic. Roumis, in this context, means Christian Soldier.

El Krim, in real life, was an Arab Rif leader in the early 20th century who was a thorn in the side of both The Legion and Spain's colonial troops in Morocco, where he tried to kick out the colonial occupiers by force, using tactics that later inspired Che Guevara and Ho Chi Minh.

Throughout this wee book, you may have come across names that you recognise from other 'Legion' films and books, that was very deliberate on my part, my way of paying tribute to Beau Geste, March or Die and even Legionnaire, and to a multitude of others pieces of Legion literature, though all I've borrowed are the names, not the actual characters.

The song 'Le Boudin' does indeed refer to the rolled up blankets on the top of Legionnaires' packs, but though the tune was widespread at the time of The Mexican Campaign, as it was originally a bugle call, the lyrics as we know them today didn't really emerge until after the Franco-Prussian War of 1870-71. Again, using the song in my wee story was by artistic license. The Mexican tune, El Deguello, was indeed a Mexican Army tune used to intimidate enemies, and it does indeed date back to the time of the Moors in Spain.

I'm amazed that there has never been a major English or any other language motion picture or TV drama about Camerone and the events surrounding it. It's a huge piece of history in the Mexican and American context, and in France it is simply France's most heroic battle and April 30th, Camerone Day, is, of course, a national holiday in France. Perhaps there's no movie because it was France's Foreign Legion, and not its regular army, who were the heroes that day, or perhaps no-one's even thought of it. I'm sure there'll be a film about it soon, hopefully a good one.

There should be – Camerone makes the 300 Spartans' stand at Thermopylae seem plain and ordinary.

France's Foreign Legion was formed in 1831 in an attempt to rid Paris of a lot of troublemaking jobless immigrants. It first fought in Algeria and in Spain's Carlist War in the 1830's, and also fought in The Crimean War of 1854-56. In Spain, The Legion fought well but suffered horrendous casualties, fighting for France on the Liberal side during Spain's Civil War of the time. In The Crimea, The Legion also fought well, as it did at France's great victory over Austria at Magenta in 1859, a battle that gave its name to the colour, Magenta.

In North-Africa , The Legion initially performed poorly and was almost scrapped a few times in its formative years, but over time, it toughened up, adapted, and became the legendary fighting force that it is today. That legend truly began in earnest at that place called Camerone in Mexico in 1863.

France's long intervention in Mexico's 'Great Argument' in the 1860's isn't one of the better known aspects of history, especially in the English speaking world, but it is nevertheless one of the most fascinating, and tragic. 'Afrancesados' is a Spanish term that originated during The Napoleonic Wars of 1808-14. It means 'those who support France'.

The Legion was sent to fight all of those foreign campaigns on behalf of France simply because the French people didn't like their own soldiers to die in foreign or colonial wars, they preferred to leave this 'dirty work' to foreigners, and that suited France's governments over the years, both Republican and Imperial, perfectly well. Foreign Wars are rarely popular at home, as events before and since Camerone have shown, so using The Legion was always of great benefit to France.

Some describe The Legion as being a mercenary force – that is simply untrue. Mercenaries fight for a certain amount of time and can easily turn on their employers if they are offered a better deal. Legionnaires were, and are, soldiers of France, not mercenaries. The Legion has always been an apolitical force too, in that France has deployed it to fight in many countries on the side of many different political forces. For example, in Spain's Carlist War, The Legion was fighting on the Liberal side, yet in Mexico, it was fighting on the right-wing side.

The one occasion that The Legion did try to directly influence French politics was The Legion's failed attempted mutiny in 1961, when it attempted to depose France's legitimate President Charles De Gaulle and install a more right-wing regime in France and Algeria, the main result of which was The Legion being downsized to just 8000 men and finally put under the direct control of France's regular army.

Legionnaires however, have come from all walks of life and have been of all political persuasions.

In the 19th century, many Irishmen joined The Legion in order to gain military experience, in preparation for a war of liberation that ultimately never came in Ireland at that time. The end of World War One saw The Legion fill with ex-German POWs or soldiers who had nothing to go home to. The global turmoil that followed the 1929 Wall Street Crash and subsequent Great Depression drew all sorts of men into The Legion, meaning that The Legion became even more cosmopolitan, comprising all sorts from anti-semitic fascist types to ideologically driven Marxists and leftists. The Spanish Civil War of 1936-39 caused many desertions in The Legion, as men from both sides of the 'argument' made for Spain to join 'their' side'. There is evidence which suggests that elements of The Legion wanted to intervene on the Republican/Liberal side in The Spanish Civil War, though France's non-intervention policy and France's own internal bickering between left and right made sure that this never happened.

The end of World War Two saw another influx of former German army recruits and veterans joining The Legion, many of them ending up fighting for France and The Legion in Indo-China.

Of course, Legionnaires enlisted for reasons other than political ones. Most were, as with most soldiers, enlisted for purely economic reasons – they needed a job, food, shelter and stability. Some enlisted because they were on the run from the law, or from a bad marriage. Some had been wounded in love and sought to vent their frustrations on distant battlefields. Some were looking for a second chance in life, and many were in it purely for the adventure. Human nature being as it is, another great 'recruiting sergeant' for The Legion was

Hollywood, particularly the film adaptations of PC Wren's 'Beau Geste', which drew hundreds of men from across the world to the colours. Many speculate that PC Wren himself was a Legionnaire in the pre-1914 Legion, for a time!

Whatever their reasons for joining or their personal background though, they were all Legionnaires, members of the finest fighting force that the world has ever seen since The Romans.

The Legion has featured in scores of English-language novels and in several English-language films.

'Beau Geste' has been made at least four times for the screen – a silent version in 1926, a black and white Hollywood version in 1939, a colour Hollywood version made in 1966, and a charming TV adaptation was made by the BBC in 1982. The BBC TV version is the only screen version which remains true to the book, with the evil Sergeant-Major Lejaune being played brilliantly by John Forgeham, and the brothers Geste played by Benedict Taylor, Jonathon Morris and Anthony Calf. For some odd reason, the 1939 Gary Cooper version of Beau Geste changes the evil sergeant's name to Markov, rather than Lejaune, as it is in the book, and only in the BBC TV version do the besieged soldiers sing 'Le Boudin' whilst under siege at the fort – one of the book's pivotal moments. In the era of Hollywood remakes, perhaps it's time for another version.

1977 saw Gene Hackman star in 'March or Die', a movie about The Legion's re-redeployment to Africa after The First World War. It's a great film and hasn't really aged, and in it The Legionnaires sing 'Le Boudin' on the march.

1998 saw the release of 'Legionnaire' starring Jean- Claude Van Damme, who also helped to produce the film. It is basically a re-hash of 'March or Die', with a boxing match and love affair replacing the initial back story from 'March or Die'. The film is entertaining, though Legion 'know-all's' might be annoyed by the fact that 'Le Boudin' is sung slightly wrongly by the marching troops in the film.

Yet still these, and other films, have no sign of Camerone. That is a shame.

Many actions in military history, particularly from the 19th Century, are seen as glorious 'last stand' battles and have been given due recognition in book, TV and film. Camerone , despite being easily the most heroic action at greatest odds, is the exception to this rule. There is no movie, no TV drama, which is a real shame. There were many great 'last stand actions' in the 1800's, I'll let you judge from these little snippets which you think was the most heroic.

20th Maine's defence of Little-Round Top at Gettysburg in July 1863 happened barely eight weeks after Camerone, and has been immortalised in film and in scores of books. It was a heroic action – Chamberlain's 20th Maine numbered fewer than 400 men and managed to fight off over 2500 Confederate soldiers who had the same rifles as them, even charging downhill at the Confederates when ammunition ran out. 20th Maine were outnumbered about 7-1, but they were not outgunned, and there were three other Union regiments to their right that could have plugged the gap had they been defeated. There were also around 75,000 other Union soldiers within a few miles, so while Chamberlain and the 20th's valiant defence and counter attack was worthy of remembrance, it is questionable whether or not their defeat would have been the disaster that many have speculated that it might have been, had they actually been defeated. At the end of the day, they weren't defeated or wiped out, they held. This in no way detracts from the courage and valour shown by both sides in the engagement, particularly when it comes to the 20th's bayonet charge.

The defence of The Alamo in 1836 is another action that has been lionised over the years, and remembered in many books and films. Like Camerone, it involved a huge Mexican regular force surrounding a much smaller enemy force inside a makeshift fortress. Colonel Travis, The Alamo's commander, had about 200 men, while the Mexicans had an army of about 3200 men, though only 1800 of them were actually needed to capture The Alamo. The Alamo is different because The 'Texian' defenders were mostly volunteers rather than regular soldiers, and were seen as pirates rather than soldiers by the besieging Mexicans, who saw the Texians as land thieves. Nevertheless, for 13 days Travis and his tiny command defied Santa Anna's Mexican Army, buying time for Sam Houston and the rest of Texas to raise and train a new army, until 1800

Mexicans stormed the makeshift fortress at dawn on March 6th 1836, killing all of its defenders. The Alamo's defenders had several artillery pieces but lacked canister shot to fire from them, limiting the effectiveness of their batteries. Only around thirty of Travis's men had bayonets and muskets, the rest of The Alamo's defenders being mostly armed with long rifles – much more accurate, but slower to load and with no bayonet socket. In contrast, every man of The Mexican assault force had either a bayonet or a sword. Travis's men deserve their place in history, for their stand awoke a nation, but they were only actually outnumbered 9-1 in the final battle. They did manage to kill or wound almost one-third of the attacking force though – an admirable achievement.

Two actions of The USA'S Plains Indian Wars are famous examples of 'last stand actions'.

The Fetterman Massacre of 1866 and the annihilation of Custer's battalion of the 7th Cavalry at the Little- Bighorn ten years later have both been written about extensively, though there's no movie about The Fetterman Massacre yet, while Custer's story has been told again and again in film and TV.

The Fetterman Massacre of December 1866 saw 80 US soldiers and two civilian guides lured into an ambush and then wiped out by around 2000 Sioux and Cheyenne warriors. The idiot Fetterman's men were armed with a mix of rifled muskets, repeating carbines, and bayonets, while the Indian force that wiped them out was armed almost exclusively with traditional weapons. Fetterman's command was outnumbered about 25-1, but was caught on an open slope and didn't last very long, nor did it take much of a toll on its enemies. This is one engagement that truly was a 'massacre' rather than a battle. Ten years later, Custer's 200 or so 7th Cavalrymen were also wiped out by about 2000 Sioux and Cheyenne , odds of 10-1, but most historians now agree that it was actually the Indians who possessed superior firepower at the Little-Bighorn, so in truth, the outcome was no surprise. In total, 265 US soldiers died at the Little-Bighorn, the majority of them with Custer's battalion, though more than half of the regiment did survive the battle. The true tragedy of these two engagements was that on both occasions the soldiers were led to their deaths by arrogant officers – the Indians who defeated them were merely defending their homes.

Egypt's humiliating defeat at the hands of the Sudanese Dervishes at The Battle of Shaykan in 1883 is the worst colonial defeat ever suffered by a 'modern' army to an indigenous force. Egypt's Army was led by Britain's Colonel William 'Billy' Hicks and ten other European officers, but its rank and file was made up of terrified Egyptian conscripts. 10,000 men, 7000 of whom were infantrymen armed with fairly modern Remington rifles. Hick's army also had several early machine guns, and was well-supplied with artillery and cavalry. However, its Achilles Heel was its morale, and after a tortuous, thirst filled march across The Sudan, it was fell upon by 40,000 screaming Dervishes in the Forest of Shaykan, near the town of El Obeid, which it was being sent to re-capture from the Dervishes. Except for Hicks, his staff, and a few hundred Bashi-Bazuks , The Egyptian soldiers, weak with thirst, went down like sheep, even though the Dervish army was armed mostly with spears, swords and sticks. Winston Churchill later called Hicks' army "The worst army that has ever marched to war". Only a few hundred Egyptians survived from the 10,000 strong force. Even then though, The Egyptians had only been outnumbered 4-1.

On the 22nd of January 1879, British forces fought two very different battles against The Zulus in South Africa, having provoked a war with the Zulus by invading their sovereign territory after the Zulus had rejected a humiliating and nigh-on impossible to comply with ultimatum from British colonial officials.

At a place called Isandlwana, around 1300 men of the British invasion force, including 800 Imperial redcoats and their colonial allies, complete with modern rifles and artillery, were attacked and annihilated by the main spear-wielding Zulu Army , which numbered 20,000, though only 15,000 of them attacked at Isandlwana. That morning, Lord Chelmsford had split the Isandlwana camp's garrison into two and promptly marched off with half of it , and had further endangered the camp's defence by dismissing HIS OWN standing orders that all camps should be entrenched. The result of this was what can perhaps be described as murder on the part of Chelmsford. The British soldiers and their colonial allies were left to die on the slopes with not enough men with which to defend the camp's huge perimeter effectively. Few white soldiers escaped, though the British redcoats did kill or wound some 3000 Zulus with their murderous rifle-fire before they were outflanked and overwhelmed – about a fifth of the Zulu attacking force. Isandlwana was a humiliation for the British, though it was not the fault of the rank and file. Had the garrison concentrated in tight formation around its ammunition supplies, rather than trying to fight The Zulus in over-stretched firing lines hundreds of yards from the camp and their precious reserve bullets, in all probability, the attack would have been easily repulsed. The British at Isandlwana were outnumbered by about 12-1. That afternoon ,over 3000 Zulus, seething at being kept out of the Isandlwana battle, disobeyed their King and attacked a tiny British force at the supply depot at Rorke's Drift. The Zulu King had not ordered this attack, and his warriors were disobeying his express order that they should not attack the British when they were in entrenched positions.

Rorke's Drift was defended by around 140 British infantrymen, from the same 24th regiment that had been destroyed at Isandlwana. They were supported by 10 colonial levies and 100 colonial irregular cavalrymen, but the cavalrymen fled the field early in the engagement, leaving the British on their own. This time The British, outnumbered 25-1, heroically beat off the Zulus, whose attack was more like a botched raid than a full-blown assault, and the terrified British defenders, having expended nearly 30,000 rounds, were able to breathe easy by morning. This was mostly down to the fact that they had built chest-high barricades.

17 British soldiers were killed, and 15 were wounded. The Zulus lost around 350 warriors killed in the actual battle, but another 500 or so wounded Zulus were clubbed or bayoneted to death after the battle. Eleven of Rorke's Drift's gritty defenders were awarded the VC as part of a PR exercise by the British government in order to try to divert attention from what had happened at Isandlwana. The 'No quarter' rule appears in most colonial battles for one simple reason – modern European or American armies, when fighting each other,

could abandon a field-hospital if they had to retreat, knowing that the enemy would take care of the wounded. When fighting people who were seen as 'savages', this was impossible, as 'savages' fought to the death, even when wounded, and did not consider a fight to be over until their enemy was dead. Add to that the fact that these 'savages' would probably be extremely angry at those who were invading their country, and would not exactly be in a charitable mood towards them, and consider the simple fact that colonial tribes didn't have the facilities or even the notion to feed and keep prisoners, and their 'savagery' seems more pragmatic. Their better armed invaders rarely took prisoners either – water, manpower and food were scarce enough for the invading armies too.

One final Colonial battle to look at is the Italian disaster at Adowa, Ethiopia, in 1896, where the Italians almost outdid Egypt's Hicks expedition of 1883 in terms of casualties. The Italians lost 7000 men , The Ethiopians 5000, but The Ethiopians were by far the more poorly equipped force.

So, we have looked at a selection of European and American 'last-stand' type actions, or actions where one side is completely annihilated.

Out of all the great 'to the last round' engagements of the 19th century, it's plain that The French Foreign Legion's stand at Camerone was both the most heroic, the most useful, and faced by far the greatest odds – 50-1. Not only were 'Danjou's Demons' outnumbered 50-1, but their enemies were better armed than them as well. Captain Danjou's command had no hope of relief or escape. They were technically destroyed by The Mexicans, the 3rd company existed no longer, but they had helped the supply convoy to get through, and had managed to fight off a whole enemy army of over 3000 men for ELEVEN HOURS, killing or wounding at least 500 Mexicans – one-sixth of the attacking force. A tactical defeat - but a strategic triumph. On hearing of Camerone, Napoleon III ordered that 'Camerone' was to be embroidered onto The Legion's flag.

On 30th April in 1954, Le Boudin was sung and Camerone Day was celebrated by The Legionnaires in their foxholes who were under siege and only one week away from defeat at Dien-Bien-Phu in Vietnam, the Legion's 'other' glorious defeat. Despite depleted supply lines , the men were able to celebrate Camerone Day with two American cigarettes per man, and some red wine.

Today there is a memorial at Camerone, and whenever troops from the nearby Mexican army base go past it, they stop to present arms, in honour of the brave men who fought and died on both sides. Individual Mexican soldiers who drive or walk past the place always stop to salute. To this day, French representatives attend annual memorial services at Camerone along with their former enemies.

The memorial in Mexico reads:

"Here there were less than sixty opposed to a whole army. Its numbers crushed them. Life rather than courage abandoned these French soldiers on April 30, 1863. In their memory, the motherland has erected this monument"

Bibliography:

Porch,Douglas –The French Foreign Legion

Brunon, Jean -Camerone.

Patay, Max -Camerone 1863.

Ryan, James W- Camerone: The French Foreign Legion's Greatest Battle

Asher, Michael – Khartoum : The Ultimate Colonial Adventure

Knight, Ian – Zulu Rising

Connel, Evan – Son Of The Morning Star

Wren, Christopher – Beau Geste